1988

The Vocal Sound

Barbara Kinsey Sable

University of Colorado

Prentice-Hall, Inc., Englewood Cliffs, New Jersey   07632

Library of Congress Cataloging in Publication Data

SABLE, BARBARA KINSEY.
  The vocal sound.

    1. Singing—Instruction and study.
MT820.S12   784.9'3   81-19224
ISBN 0-13-942979-4   AACR2

Design and editorial/
  production supervision by
  Chrys Chrzanowski
Interior layout by Gail Collis
Cover design by Jayne Conte
Manufacturing buyer: Harry P. Baisley

Printed in the United States of America

10 9 8 7 6 5 4 3

ISBN 0-13-942979-4

PRENTICE-HALL INTERNATIONAL, INC., *London*
PRENTICE-HALL OF AUSTRALIA PTY. LIMITED, *Sydney*
PRENTICE-HALL OF CANADA, LTD., *Toronto*
PRENTICE-HALL OF INDIA PRIVATE LIMITED, *New Delhi*
PRENTICE-HALL OF JAPAN, INC., *Tokyo*
PRENTICE-HALL OF SOUTHEAST ASIA PTE. LTD., *Singapore*
WHITEHALL BOOKS LIMITED, *Wellington, New Zealand*

Contents

chapter xi

Listening for the Vocal Sound **64**

chapter xii

Phrasing **69**

Songs Included: *Dundee; Die Armen Will der Herr Umarmen; Es halt' es mit der blinden Welt; Gerechter Gott, ach, rechnest Du; Wie rafft ich mich auf; Bid Me to Live* (some are excerpts)

chapter xiii

The Text **78**

chapter xiv

Repertoire **83**

Songs Included: *Sorgi Candida Aurora; I'm Nobody; Fog* (some are excerpts)

Songs with Accompaniment

* Lower key provided for this song

Preface

Voice classes and private voice students come in many sizes, descriptions, and experiences. Backgrounds differ, potentials differ, and, most importantly, goals differ. It is rare for any given voice class to be so homogeneous that a teacher can individualize all of the subject matter. Some students have already had some voice training, some are lucky if they are able to produce a tone, some are actors striving to produce saleable tones, some have to take voice in order to obtain certification, and some have longed to get some vocal training. Some read music well; others don't, and so on. The teacher faced with leading different voices to better tones also has to fulfill the varying needs of the class. If this were the best of all worlds, it might be possible by stringent auditioning to at least start with voice classes that were homogeneous. But economics and time being what they are, ideal situations seldom exist.

The classroom voice teacher, as well as the teacher of beginning private students, therefore has the problem of presenting to many individuals the "beginnings" of a variety of subject matter pertaining to the development of vocal sound. It would be nice in such circumstances to have one source book in the hands of the entire class. The contents should lead students to more advanced material. It should be organized to enable the student to find his or her particular needs, and those needs ought to be presented in a fashion that is not insulting to the intelligence of the average student. With this in mind, THE VOCAL SOUND introduces many topics: diction, history of art song, technique, phrasing, the handling of text, exercises, practicing, and listening. This allows the teacher to spend more time teaching voice and less time gathering materials for the varied assortment of student needs.

Voice students often feel that the schooling of the voice is intensely internal, and that there is little material that can be grasped. It is true that singing is deeply personal. It involves muscles and feelings that each of us experiences in a different manner. Consequently, the questions and the needs of voice students do not occur in an organized way. Therefore, if the student has in his hands a book that has the bases of a good number of subjects relative to vocal training, he is able to find answers to questions. In this book the answers do not pretend to cover the subject deeply; they are introductory. But they are also introductions that give references that will further the students' search for knowledge. Students are encouraged to go further into the subjects presented. They are urged to read through the material so that they begin to understand the immensity of the singing process. If they are aware of the various skills they must obtain, they can allow those skills to grow with them from their first vocal experiences. Then they will not be so apt to stumble upon some entirely unknown skill that will suddenly need to be developed.

The first chapter of the book, "The Essentials of Vocal Technique," is designed for all students as a guide to the discussions concerning the handling of the voice. Later sections can be assigned as the teacher sees fit or as the student feels impelled to explore. Many new students have no idea, for instance, what repertoire is available for them to sing, nor do they know how to apply the theory of music to their voice lessons. The lessons described are guides for beginners to use in order to set up the disciplines with which they are going to have to deal. Once they have ordered their practicing, their thinking about vocal tone, and their ability to phrase, they will be able to grow as singers.

Lesson plans, therefore, can develop from the use of the book in terms of the needs of each particular group of students. The book is designed to allow the teacher to guide the learning process, using his or her imagination and ability. For instance, the chapter on Practice Routine is a guide that can be assigned for outside use. Exercises can be used as the teacher feels they best fit any particular situation. The material on diction can be made to fit the situation; that is, it can be used in its entirety by classes and students who are required to sing in foreign languages or it can be given limited use in those situations oriented toward English. The latter would prove particularly helpful in those cases where one or two students in a group otherwise directed wish to sing in German or Italian.

Thus, the multiplicity of the book will fill in the various gaps in the assorted backgrounds of many students. Too frequently, harried voice teachers are apt to conclude that a voice that sings fairly well "knows" quite a bit. That is often not the truth. Such a student reading through this manual will find knowledge that is new to him and ideas he has not been taught. At least, he will be able to ask questions about his deficit learning.

Students find it very difficult to learn how to listen to their own voices. It is hoped that every student will come quickly to the point where he or she does indeed hear the sound of his fellow students, and then his or her own sound. Voice classes have their particular glory in that they provide a place for the student to listen to many vocal sounds. However, one of the places where a student often fails to practice his ability to listen to that sound is, oddly enough, in the practice room. Here, confronted with a piano, the student will often bathe in sound of the piano accompaniment and never once think of the vocal line as a source of pure sound. Consequently, the songs presented throughout the book are presented without piano accompaniments. Full bibliographic material is provided so that such accompaniments may be found if necessary. A number of canons are also given in order to acquaint the student with the sound of solo voices singing in parts. This is a skill that most singers cultivate, and this is a fine place to begin that skill.

The importance of an accessible text with bibliographies for further study is that it allows each teacher to develop a technique for teaching his or her ideas and concepts. A book cannot teach anyone to sing. Sometimes a book can remind the singer of fundamentals. Sometimes it can give reasons and explanations. Sometimes it can direct the singer to sources where she can find additional information. Sometimes a book can even awaken curiosity, or goad a student to do more work. No great revelations are made here. No definitive answers are presented. Ways are suggested.

Barbara Kinsey Sable

chapter i

The Essentials of Vocal Technique

The most available instrument, both economically and geographically, is the voice. One may not be able to afford a grand piano or a flute, but the voice is there. Since involvement in the arts is important if appreciation is to follow, the accessibility of the voice as an instrument should bring more people into contact with music. It is quite essential that this involvement be knowledgeable, that it include standards for vocal technique as well as for the vocal sound. Such involvement will eventually produce better singing, better music, and happier experiences for the ears of our neighbors.

Voice students must learn to teach themselves. More time is spent in the practice room alone than with a teacher. Therefore, students are their own teachers most of the time. They must know what a good sound is while they are producing one, and they must know how it feels to produce such a sound. This is not easy, for singers hear their own voices through bone conduction, whereas others hear them through air conduction. This fact makes the learning process a long one. Students must train their ears to hear sound from the reference point of their teacher's ears. There will come a time when students should recognize a few concrete feelings and hear some sounds that they know are correct. It is of great value to at least know when one is right. Singers are their own instruments, and therefore it is extremely difficult to hear the sound as it is being produced. It can be felt, and ears can be trained to hear as others hear. That process is a long one.

The properly produced vocal sound is free, warm, resonant, and capable of agility and dynamic change. In order to understand this sound, students should be able to listen to their own voices as well as those of others. Without this ability no real progress will take place. It is hoped that the following comments will help the student to find good sound and to recognize it, for it is sound that the vocal student must produce in order to discover how to approach problems of vocal production.

THE ESSENTIALS IN BRIEF

Posture. The singer should stand straight but not stiffly, feet slightly apart and not parallel, shoulders relaxed, the weight of the shoulders and the head resting on a midpoint of the back without tension. The ears are approximately over the shoulder seams of the clothing. The body feels buoyant. The lowest two ribs remain slightly up and out throughout the breathing process.

Reservoir. Although air is obviously stored in the lungs, there is a feeling of expansion between the waistband and the bottom two ribs — the floating ribs — which grows when breath is taken properly. This area is held out and up by the intercostal muscles coupled with the interaction of many other back muscles and the action of the diaphragm. Singers should learn the feeling of the proper balance of these abdominal muscles, and learn to rely upon the feeling of support and width that they can give. The diaphragm automatically descends upon inhalation. The singer is concerned with the rate of its return, an action controlled by the pressure exerted from the contents of the abdominal cavity.

Pump. This is the steady stream of air maintained by the action of the abdominal muscles and the *nonaction* of the muscles in the collarbone region. The abdominal muscles — the rectus abdominis, external oblique (right and left), internal oblique (right and left), transversus abdominis, intercostals, and back muscles, including the latissimus dorsi — are used partially for breath control and partially for support of the entire vocal mechanism. This support, when properly attained, gives the body the sensation of floating. There is a balancing of factors that includes little tension at the neck and throat area and great support, without extreme tension, from the lower part of the body.

Phonation. Sound is made at the level of the vocal cords. The cords sound with a complicated system of adjustments that are modified from the extreme "heavy" adjustment using the wide and full cords at the bottom of the range to the "light" adjustment using thin chords for higher tones. Often the falsetto uses less of the thin chords, a process called *dampening*. Singers are also aware of a sensation in their facial structure. Generally, but not by all people, this sensation is felt in the area of the bridge of the nose. It seems as though the tone actually starts from this placement and then connects with a sound from the larynx. Such tones have a brilliant "ring" to them. They do not feel as though they were made in the throat, nor do they have undue throat tension.

Resonance. After the sound has been made, it is filtered and strengthened so that it may be projected and heard. Part of this process is the production of the "ringing" sound discussed above. It is believed that the three main resonators of sound are the pharynx, the nasopharynx, and the mouth. Other resonators may exist, but these three are fairly well agreed upon by vocal scientists, and they offer sufficient explanation for the coloring and production of good tone to be of value to the singer.

Diction. Vowels are produced by varying shapes of the three resonators. Consonants are produced by a freely moving tongue and articulate lips.

The Ear. Continual training of the ear is essential, for the ear monitors and corrects both the conscious and unconscious processes of vocal production.

DEFINITIONS

Breath support. This is the ability to maintain the rib cage in an easy high position, without the use of shoulder tension, against the pull of gravity.

Breath control. This is the ability to regulate the exhalation of air by the abdominal muscles, again without undue tension through the high chest area and the throat.

THE ESSENTIALS IN DEPTH

Vocal production is based on the skill of handling breath support and breath control in balance with proper phonation. Without a steady stream of breath there will be little good tone, and without the proper support for the stream of breath the singer will use muscle tension that will ultimately strangle her tone quality. The process of breathing must be dealt with at all levels of voice production. As the body matures, and as the sound of the singer improves, she must restudy the quantity and the quality of her breathing and pay attention to the continual rebalancing of resonation and support. This means fairly constant attention to a very basic problem. Often such problems are slighted because of the boredom of the mechanics involved. It therefore behooves the student to demand that periodic attention be given to her breathing problems both in the practice room and in the studio.

Posture

Breathing begins with good posture. The spine should be straight (remember, the spine continues into the head), the hollow of the back as flat as possible, and the rib cage not permitted to sag. Singers are their own instruments. This means that the vitality of their tone quality is related to the vitality of their bodies. *Vitality is not tension.* Muscle tonicity is essential to good tone. Tension, over clutched muscles, will destroy good tone. The rib cage is floated up from the bottom: the muscles of the shoulders and the neck (the pectoralis major, the subclavius, and the others) should not be tense. The head should be in line with the spine, not jutting outward or held tightly back. The weight of the head and the shoulders rests on a point on the spine about five inches below the shoulders, or at least it should seem so. The feet should be apart, and not on the same parallel, for unless they are uneven there is a great tendency to seesaw on the stage. Body weight should be distributed evenly on the feet. Some people find it necessary to put a bit more weight on the back foot. Singers often have the feeling that their weight is balanced on the ball of the foot, a position that gives vitality to the entire body.

The body should have an easy and energetic feeling of lift to it around the waist. The feeling is akin to that of a good stretch.

Breathing

It should be a very simple thing to take a breath. However, many singers are so tight, so nervous, and so overly concerned with technique that they commit many vocal errors before they sing their first note. Granted good and easy posture with the upper torso relaxed, the air passes through a completely free throat into the lungs. This action presses the diaphragm down without help from any voluntary muscles. Now the singer should be prepared to let the air out. If he is tense in the region of the neck, upper chest, or throat, the air will be held back instead of carrying tone. The tension in the upper chest may be an unfortunate reminder that the larynx was not created only for phonation, but also as an aid for lifting. Heavy lifting requires a closure of the vocal ligaments and the use of abdominal muscles. These abdominal muscles are also used when we sing, and the result is that we often cannot disassociate abdominal and upper-torso muscles. When this happens a "tight" singing tone is sounded. It is a learned discipline to approximate the cords without the tension needed for lifting. The breathing process includes the posture needed to sing. There is a feeling of lift around the waistband and just above it that helps the larynx achieve the proper adjustment for tones that are outside of the middle range — the very low and the very high. This lift is felt particulary in the back at the spine between the fixed rib cage and the fixed pelvic bones. The location of the sway back is a fairly good description of its position. An outward and upward stance here, including the floating ribs, will give additional support to the tones, help them to find the "ring" that seems to occur in the upper face, and allow the voice to mix its registers properly. A *register* is defined as all those notes that use the same mechanism at the level of the larynx. This definition, though a handy one, is coming under critical scrutiny from some investigators who wonder if each note isn't produced somewhat differently from all the other notes. Consequently, it might be better to define those tones that seem to be produced in a like manner, and produce like sounds, as one register.

In order for the body to receive air, the diaphragm, a willing servant with no proprioceptive nerve endings and consequently not subject to willed direction, descends. Proper exhalation for singing is achieved by the slow ascent of the diaphragm. This ascent results from the pressure of the contents of the abdominal cavity. The body must have a good stance in order to give unrestricted passage for this process. It will be found that muscles in the lower abdominal area and the gluteus muscles will be somewhat active in order to permit this slow ascent. Singers should periodically check their rib cages, to make sure that they remain in an easy, high position during both exhalation and inhalation. This support for the thorax must come from the intercostal muscles, not the shoulder muscles. Again, it will help to have the hollow of the back as flat as it can be with a little pressure toward the outside wall—a *little* pressure, for too much will tie the singer in knots. The lower two ribs of the thorax expand as air is taken, and the conscious effort to maintain this outward and upward expansion as long as possible during exhalation helps maintain adequate support. Actually this is a psychological gesture more than a physiological one, but if the thorax is allowed to be squeezed too quickly, breath is lost without proper use and the thorax drops. This expansion also helps maintain the feeling of lift in the torso that helps achieve tone quality that is even throughout the scale. When the thorax is allowed to drop, the singer has to gasp for the next breath.

The rhythm of breathing ought to become habitual: an open throat, then inhalation, followed by a sigh that carries the singing tone outward. Open throat—breathe—sigh (sing) out with no catches during the entire cycle, whether a catch in the throat or in the breathing apparatus.

If the sigh seems to start from a high position in the nose, even above the bridge of the nose—just as a siren (in the regular voice, not the falsetto) sound starts—the singer will find that he has the correct ring in his sound as well as little tension in the throat. Sometimes this sound can be found through humming with loose but closed lips and a very resonant feeling in the nose. Sliding from a siren tone into a regular tone is an excellent way of finding the sound in question. This sound will help to establish the breathe—sigh—sing cycle, for it is produced with no catch in it and should be used as the basis for a good singing tone.

Once the singer has some feeling for the breathing process he should attempt to pinpoint the sensations in and about the nose so that they may become a focal point for the sound. This set of vibrations gives a ring to the voice that is necessary for the production of a tone that will carry through and above an orchestra. It also gives the tone a vitality that no manner of "miking" can replace. This placement is found differently by each singer. The siren, already mentioned, plus the following suggestions may be helpful:

1. The "sniff place."[1]
2. The snoring or snarling place.
3. Above the *ng* sound in *sing*.
4. A nasal placement without a nasal sound. Suggestion: Sing on a nasal *ng* then open to a natural sound using the same placement. What the layman terms *nasality* is actually the closing off of the nasopharynx from the pharynx. What the singer is striving for here is to free the nasopharynx from tension.
5. The placement one uses when surprised into shouting "Hey!" to someone in the distance.

There are more. Remember to check breathing habits at the same time, for the two go together.

One can expect to find motion at the bottom of the rib cage, at the sides, and at the back at the time of inspiration. There should be no upward movement in the upper chest. Such movement generally means that either the chest has been too high before inspiration or that it is laced with tight muscles in the shoulder region.[2]

Phonation

Once the diaphragm has begun its ascent the vocal sound can be produced. A steady, controlled stream of air going between vocal folds that are allowed to vibrate freely produces a good vocal sound. The action of the vocal folds is myoelastic-aerodynamic—that is, determined by breath and muscle tension. Breath produces sound by the Bernoulli effect.[3] The muscles required to create vocal tension in the folds are really below the level of consciousness and can best be controlled by the ear.

It is a *steady* stream of air that makes good vocal tone. (The actual amount of air is not as great as one might expect. It does not necessarily take large amounts of air to sing, merely well-used air.) This stream is already controlled to some extent by the maintenance of a strong and flexible reservoir, by a good and easy stance, and by an upright rib cage that includes no tension in the shoulder area.

If the upper abdominal muscles are quickly and forcefully pushed in, air is jutted out. These muscles are used at first with a strong, vital movement. With further discipline the movement becomes more subtle. This push should be coupled with absolute relaxation of the throat and neck. It is similar to a laugh, the belly laugh of a small child, for instance. With this motion the singer can steadily throw air upward without involving muscles in the upper part of the body. That is, the singer can use the abdominal muscles without interfering with the relaxation of the shoulder and throat muscles. Such use requires active muscles, *not tense* muscles. The abdominal muscles can also assist in the formation of consonants by providing energy for the movement of the tongue so that power does not come from the tension at the root of the tongue. With the use of this explosion of power from below, and with just the tip of the tongue used for articulation, the tongue need not be tight when producing consonants or vowels; it can move freely and return to a resting position at the base of the lower gums without tension.

The muscles of the larynx and the throat are connected with other muscles in the jaw, tongue, and lips. These muscles must not be unduly tensed if proper resonation is to take place. The jaw has a double hinge action: it can swing out or downward. In singing, only the downward motion should be allowed. In fact, the higher tones are best approached by a downward and inward motion of the jaw.

---

[1]See Lucie Manen, *The Art of Singing* (London: Faber Music, 1974; Bryn Mawr: Theodore Presser, 1976), pp. 27-8.

[2]See Frederick Husler and Yvonne Rodd-Marling, *Singing: The Physical Nature of the Vocal Organ* (London: Faber & Faber, 1965), pp. 30-51.

[3]William Vennard, *Singing: The Mechanism and the Technic*, 4th ed. (New York: Carl Fischer, 1967), p. 39.

Resonance and Diction

It is absolutely essential if proper resonance—that is, proper amplification of the sound—is to be expected that freedom from muscular tension in the tongue and throat be a goal. In the process of diction the tongue should be free rather than locked with tension, free but moving in a very clipped and vital way. Actual sounds are held on vowels, without any tension in the tongue, while consonants are performed as quickly and as forcefully as possible. One cannot sing words with a completely inactive tongue, but one cannot sing good tones with a tense tongue. When thinking about tension in the tongue, start with the part of the tongue that goes up when you swallow. This is a place where tension sneaks into our speaking voice and therefore into the singing voice.

A difficult block for the singer to overcome is the sensation of lack of control that he feels the first time he permits himself to sing a phrase with a completely loose jaw and tongue (particularly the end of a long phrase). It takes courage to let the jaw go as the breath departs, but it is only with that courage that a singer can discover his deeper support and the feeling of a completely free tone. If the jaw is tight, all the work that is done by the abdominal muscles is for nought, for the jaw tension will cut off the connection between resonation and airstream. At the area of the vocal folds, remember, sound is made. This sound is amplified and probably filtered in many ways, many of which are not yet documented. However, it is generally conceded that the sound is resonated in three areas: the mouth, the pharynx, and the nasopharynx. These three resonators are coupled at the point where the tongue goes up when you swallow. Resonators must respond to the original sound produced by the larynx and to changes in their shapes that make the production of vowel sounds. There is a tendency on the part of singers to support their sound by tensing the tongue and the neck muscles. Such tension makes it difficult for the laryngeal functions to take place freely and for vowel sound to occur naturally.[4] The tongue is not only a part of our diction, but our diction is very much a part of our general behavior pattern

and tensions. Therefore, it is very difficult to know when the tongue is really free. Both tension habits and nervousness, particularly during performance, are hard to overcome, and that is what the singer must do. The movement of the abdominal muscles, when not overdone, the strength a disciplined singer finds in the flank and backward movement of the lower rib cage, and the ability to "float" the rib cage without tight shoulder, neck, and tongue tensions, in time provides the right type of support so that the unwanted tensions in the tongue and elsewhere can be eliminated. At this point the jaw will also relax and the young singer will discover that although singing with a relaxed jaw seems to be a lack of control, in reality it is merely an end of overcontrol.

Voice students have often heard that they should maintain an open throat. It is very true that such a position gives maximum resonance. The singer strives for an open throat, one that is not tense in the finding of its opening, and a relaxed larynx, one that is not held in an unduly high position. The actual positioning of the pharnyx and larynx is dependent upon pitch and vowel. With an open throat, however, the produced tone per se is apt to be a "woofy," "muddy," or "hooty" sound that will not carry and has no particular ring or point to it. The addition of focus through the muscles of the upper lip (too much attention to the lower lip presents the danger of tightened jaw muscles) can correct the sound. Students frequently have to use facial contortions to find out where these muscles are, for as Americans we have extremely lazy speech habits and often do not use our lips at all. Once these muscles are found and disciplined, the contortions must be omitted so that the sound will be produced without grimaces. Sometimes if the corners of the mouth are brought in slightly, and there is a slight upward and outward motion to the under part of the upper lip, the sound will immediately assume a proper vitality. Pouting, puckering, or whistling can be used to find the proper muscles. Basses who have a greater quantity of hearable overtones and need to cut down on this number in order to produce quality will find this simple device is often the answer. "Smile" is not. To the very young, "smile" often means pull your mouth back as far as it will go and tighten your neck muscles. All too frequently it can result in a spread tone that cannot convey authority to the audience.

---

[4]See Richard Luchsinger and Godfrey Arnold, *Voice, Speech, Language*, trans. Evelyn Robe Finkbeimer (Belmont, Calif.: Wadsworth, 1965) pp. 27-33.

High notes should not be supported by a tight tongue. This chief offender of so many singing ills can often be found tightening its way as singers aim for the height of their range. The larynx should be allowed to assume a low position. This position will be slightly lower than the position of the larynx at rest, but it should not be assumed too forcefully. An easy larynx position is needed particularly for high notes. This free opening then gives the maximum amount of pharyngeal resonance, and freedom for the vocal cords to make adjustments as the pitch climbs.

Vocal-Cord Adjustments

The adjustments of the vocal ligaments for actual pitch are quite complex, and not completely known as yet. It is believed that every pitch and every dynamic level is produced by a different combination of adjustments. These adjustments have two extremes: a thick, heavy meeting of the cords associated with low tones, and a thin, light meeting of the cords associated with high and light tones. The myoelastic-aerodynamic theory claims that the muscles in the vocal folds produce the low, loud tones whereas the high tones are produced mainly by the air flowing through the smaller or thinner cords. The vocalis muscle is active in low tones and loud tones. There is a combination of factors involving the crico-thyroid muscles, which contract and elongate the thyroid arytenoid to maintain pitch, and the arytenoid muscles at the rear of the larynx, which function to tighten so that the elongated and tilted vocalis muscle will approximate and produce high and light tones. Some tones can be produced in more than one manner.[5] The more obvious of these tones occur around the tones singing teachers refer to as a "break" in the voice.

It is the development of a continuous basic sound throughout the entire range that is the aim of the voice student. Even though one may be able to produce several different sounds on any note, the aim of the student is to produce one consistent sound throughout her range. The tone may be colored from time to time with different qualities,

but the coloring should be consistent with the characteristic sound of the voice throughout its range and dynamic levels. All singers of note have a number of sounds to their credit, but they all start from one basic sound. Good singers do not sing duets with themselves, much less trios.

In general, even low or loud tones should start from the light adjustment. Teachers are apt to refer to this phenomenon as the "lift" in the voice. This attitude produces the ability for agility as well as a tone that is focused or bright. It can be thought of as the clutch in a gearshift operation. In order to reach the light adjustment of the cords needed for high tones, the clutch, or "lift," must be engaged prior to the breaking point in order not to strip the gears. Some students feel a pronounced lifting in the palatal region when they achieve this tone. The ability to start low tones with a "lift" will also keep the unnecessary "wobble" out of the voice. Added to this consideration should be the warning that all high tones should start softly. They may quickly become loud, but they should start from a soft position so as to aid the cords in finding the light adjustment.

The Importance of Balance

Voice production is a balance of breath control and breath support with the method of phonation. This balance must be checked often as the singer progresses and matures. Therefore the student should not be dismayed at conflicting remarks made in any two lessons by a teacher. Balance requires manipulation on both sides of the scale. In order to establish one habit or to break another, the student is often taught to overdo; he must then relearn as he brings the sound into balance. This is also true in the training of the extreme adjustments of the vocal ligament. Many students have used one side of the set of adjustments to an extreme. The other side has to be trained and balanced and then balanced within the total sound requirements. At first this can produce a very "breathy" sound. Be not dismayed, for through the use of the extremities of both adjustments the muscles can be trained, and through the coupling of this training with the breathing apparatus, the problems will disappear. Falsetto (in the male voice) should also be practiced—not bellowed or shrieked, but used.

[5]John Large and Thomas Shipp, "The Effect of Certain Parameters on the Perception of Vocal Registers," *NATS Bulletin,* 26, No. 1 (October 1969), 12.

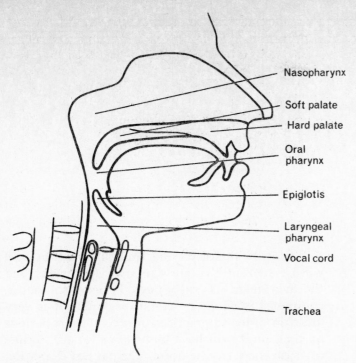

Nasopharynx

Soft palate

Hard palate

Oral pharynx

Epiglotis

Laryngeal pharynx

Vocal cord

Trachea

Fig. 1. The head and neck

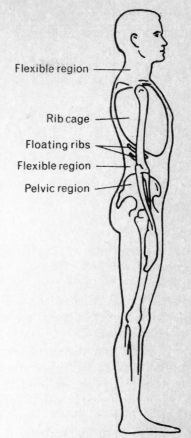

Flexible region

Rib cage

Floating ribs

Flexible region

Pelvic region

Fig. 2. Posture

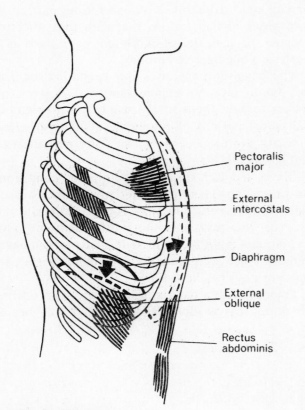

Pectoralis major

External intercostals

Diaphragm

External oblique

Rectus abdominis

Fig. 3. The rib cage

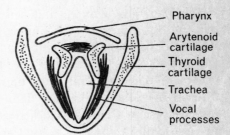

Pharynx

Arytenoid cartilage

Thyroid cartilage

Trachea

Vocal processes

Fig. 4. The vocal cords

Fig. 5. The tongue

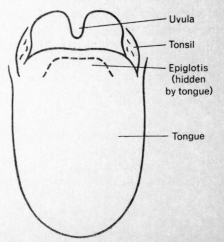

Uvula

Tonsil

Epiglotis (hidden by tongue)

Tongue

chapter ii

The Practice Routine

Many students do not know how to begin their practice sessions. Basically they should begin by searching for a good tone and then continuously strive for a better one. Each singer develops her own formula. Some type of very resonant *light* sound should be found at the beginning of each session, with no particular demands for range. A forward "mmmmm" with the lips wet and lightly closed, the teeth slightly parted, and the tongue absolutely loose may help a voice fogged with early morning to find itself. Light singing is a must until all the muscles have awakened and full support can be expected from them. The muscles of the lips can be exercised away from tone. We are such lazy speakers in this country that it is a good idea to move the lips around before singing so that you know they are working. It also helps to tighten every muscle in your throat and chest area so that you will recognize the ones that must be relaxed when you are singing. Many of us have habits so intense that these muscles are held in a rigid position without our conscious knowledge. By tightening them, then letting them relax one by one, a knowledge of the muscle placement is gained that permits one to be more conscious of their presence and to realize where they are, in order to relax them.

Singing is a muscular process. Such disciplines demand time, consistent practice, and constant effort to improve. Five hours today and nothing tomorrow will not do the trick. Progress at best will be uneven. You are your own instrument, and the instrument has rusty days. Fatigue is a factor, endurance is another. At the beginning it is very much in order to practice for several short periods of time until you have built up endurance. Bouts of frustration are the norm. The days of exaltation make them almost worthwhile.

A "bad" lesson is not *always* a bad thing. Sometimes more may be learned than when you are singing well! *Sometimes!* A bad lesson, particularly a series of bad lessons that earn that adjective because of insufficient work on your part, is a waste of your time and money.

The beginning exercises and beginning songs in this book have no accompaniments. There is no reason to sing them sitting at a piano. Remember that short periods of practicing at full concentration are more successful than long periods with half a mind.

Illness and lack of sleep are not good conditions for practicing. There are times when your physical being forbids vocal practice. These are the days to practice the text and the music mentally. This technique should be perfected, since one can never practice voice as frequently as he or she wishes because of physical limitations.

Practice with a daily routine. Here is an outline of things to be done and sounds to be heard.

Practice Routine

A. Establishing muscular alertness:
   1. Posture (stretching helps).
   2. Deep breathing.
   3. Activating the pump with short, vital muscle strokes in the abdominal region.

4. Alert phonation: Look for the high placement for the resonant tone by stretching and pinching the muscles in that region (sniff, snort, snore—anything that helps you).
5. Diction: Use the lip muscles until they have responded. Move the jaw up and down; chew.
6. Relax: neck, chest, tongue, and jaw.
7. More physical activity, silently: Stretch, particularly the spine.

B. Tonal Response:
1. Listen for a free tone.
2. Listen for an even tone with matching and sustained vowels.
3. Listen for a ringing tone.
4. Listen for a steady stream of air, in and out, that does not clutch at the moment of inhalation or exhalation.
5. Attempt to widen your ability to sustain legato phrases and long phrases.
6. Listen for correct pitch. Pitch may be wrong because of a wrong note, improper breath support, tension, or inadequate ring in the sound. Check your posture, breath support, tongue tension, jaw, and shoulder muscles.
7. Agility:
    a. Even quality in tone and dynamics.
    b. Ability to do staccato without throat tension (start from the high facial placement).
    c. Clean articulation with proper attention to breath support and clean vowels.
8. *Messa di voce:* a note crescendoed and decrescendoed without a loss of the basic tone quality. The ability to do this on a steady stream of air is fundamental to good singing.

C. Learning the Music
1. Rhythm: the beat, the tempo and the drive for each piece.
2. Pitch.
3. Composer's comments.
4. Text.
5. Memorize: *Remember, a piece is just beginning to be understood when it is memorized.*

D. Emotions:
1. Musical connotations.
2. Demands of the text.

E. Performance:
1. Standardizing without spoiling the freshness.
2. Singing a version "in"—that is, practicing until it is completely yours.
3. Practice performance (with alternate sets of breathing for emergencies such as nerves!).

F. Final practicing:
1. Learn the music all over again with an accompanist.
2. Learn to perform with the accompanist, changing in your performance habits any expressions and thoughts that may be out of character now that someone else has added her concept of the music to yours.
3. Put away the music and let it rest.
4. After a space of time—weeks, months, years, depending on the time available—start all over again.

A Typical Practice Session

1. Warm-ups so that the body will awaken:
    a. Stretch and move the body about.
    b. Fast, light scales: An octave plus one and down again is a good exercise because it is rhythmically well structured. A rhythmical setting provides the body with more opportunity to assume the correct coordination. It is not necessary to sing long periods of warm-ups. The body should be taught to respond quickly to the waking-up procedure.
2. Check on posture. Do some deep breathing and be concerned that the abdominal muscles are sending out a stream of air. Be sure that the shoulders are resting freely and that the throat muscles are not tense.

3. Tone quality: Start with an exercise that alternates rest and sound. During the rest periods, strive to find the high placement and to prepare a slide out from that place for the sound. The throat should not be tense. However, it should also not be so relaxed that it cannot function. Begin scales from the top down, starting in a comfortable portion of your range. Slowly sing them, matching each tone to the tone above. Do exercises in the next chapter.

4. Agility: Start with exercise 10 in the next chapter. Portions of your practice sessions should include difficult and very difficult fast passages. Do not become discouraged if they do not go perfectly. Stop practicing them when frustration overcomes patience.

5. If the voice now feels "right," this may be the place to attempt to sing a fairly well known song, one you have memorized, or nearly so. Listen to the tone quality. Perhaps some of it is ailing. If this is so, use that portion of the piece as an exercise until it is in line.

6. When the tone quality of this piece has been corrected, continue. Otherwise, find the appropriate exercise and practice until the difficulty has been overcome. If the problem is one of degree—for example, not enough agility or not enough control—work until you feel you have accomplished as much as is possible for the time being. Do not press your endurance or your patience past the point of being able to deal with the situation. There is a lot more to be learned.

7. Tackle a new piece of music. Play it through. Decide on the form. Read the text. Discover if you need help with the diction. If so, note what is necessary so that you may ask questions at your next lesson. What is the basic sentiment of the text? What are the musical difficulties? Can you resolve the rhythmic problems before you sing a note? Can you pull difficult pitch or vocal problems out of context and use them as exercises?

8. Try a piece that you have been working on. Perhaps it would be a good idea to listen to someone else's version, or several versions in the library at your next listening session. Sing the song, and correct musical problems. Think through the text, and be particularly conscious of the composer's intentions. Repeat the text. Is your diction accurate? Have you checked with the dictionary and used International Phonetic Alphabet symbols to correctly transcribe the sounds of the diction? How would you speak the text? Are you singing it that way, and if not, why?

9. Start to memorize a piece you have worked on for some time.

10. Continue memorizing pieces where you have already started the process.

11. Stop singing, and either go to the library to listen or silently study new scores and silently memorize old ones.

12. Start practicing all over again. This time, since you have already sung the day into a start, begin with exercises that are a little bit too much for you to do well. Sing the piece you just started today. Try to see how far you have progressed with the memorization work that is in progress.

13. If everything is going badly, sing the one piece (every singer has one) that always goes well for you, and see if you can change the temporary depression you have worked yourself into. It might be a good idea to try to figure out why this song always works and the others don't.

14. Do not practice too long, or when you are so out of patience with yourself that nothing works. This is the time to do something else and there are many other things to be done: language improvement, listening lessons, and studying of scores.

15. At least once during the day, sing something you like to sing because you like to sing it. Sing it well, and enjoy the fact that you can.

REMEMBER

Progress is made in accordance with the student's insight into the tonal and physical demands of voice and music. This requires mental alertness. Physical demands cannot be achieved by thinking about them. Practice is essential, and no one can do it for you.

Repertoire follows work. No student is ready for new repertoire until he has done something with the old.

Day-by-day progress is extremely slow. Singing is a muscular discipline and demands consistent training over long periods of time to be effective. Consequently, it is more pleasant to think of one's growth in terms of months rather than days. Do not be discouraged by setbacks. You are your own instrument, and there are times when your instrument will be severely out of tune. The goal is to make your worst singing of a high enough quality to be acceptable. This takes time, encouragement, and faith.

It is not enough to try to follow these rules in solo practice. Most voice students belong to a choir. Rules that apply to a singer's solo practice apply to choral practice also. For instance, it is very silly to practice an extremely tired choir. To do so is to practice more mistakes than good vocal tone. It is also very easy to sing with an increasingly tight throat as one sight-reads music. This is a time to sing at half voice and as relaxed as possible.

Remember most of all that it is fairly easy to sing on "good" days, when the sun is bright, grades are high, and the planets are all in the right places. A professional must sing well on her "bad" days. It is difficult when things are going wrong. No voice teacher can make up that difference in self-faith, especially for all students at all times. Expect some days of little confidence, and perhaps students and teachers can learn to store up some of the "good times" in order to carry them through the bad. But it is most important to see that you do not develop the habit of expecting someone else to be your confidence and your will.

chapter iii

Exercises

Exercises are not magic potions that if invoked enough times, will produce guaranteed results. The best exercises are those a singer creates himself in order to cure a weakness he has discovered. Then the exercise makes sense. To sing an exercise just because that is what voice students do makes no sense. The singer must know why he is singing, what it should sound like, and what it does sound like (remembering that he does not hear his voice as others do). There is harm in using exercises with no insight into their purposes, for the singer may be merely practicing his mistakes.

It is absolutely useless to do an exercise unless you know why you are doing it, or unless you have been told to do it enough times that the reason becomes obvious. In the latter instance the reason is at least obvious to your teacher. Therefore, let us put exercises into several categories. First of all are exercises that are for single functions, or that may be used to determine what single function is out of focus. Such exercises might be termed "crutches." Crutches are fine to help through a difficult period, but there comes a time when they must be thrown away. These "crutches" include:

1. Singing with your hands stretched upwards while standing on your toes. *Cause:* rib cage fell during improperly sung phrase.
2. Singing on a neutral vowel such as [ae] or [ɛ]. *Cause:* overuse of tongue and jaw in diction.
3. Singing with your head down so that you can look between your knees without holding your head stiffly. *Cause:* tensing of neck or shoulders.

(In each instance it is to be supposed that a particular phrase in the literature did not "go" well. If this phrase is then sung with the following suggestions and the resulting tone is correct, one may assume the cause of failure to be the first cause described.)

Most of these crutches are simple. Somehow, in the extremities of learning technique we are apt to forget very basic techniques. Generally it is the failure to remember lesson one that leaves lesson fifty a failure. Therefore, let us begin with a set of extremely rudimentary exercises. It is not necessary for a student to stay on one exerc e until she masters it before proceeding to the next. No exercise is ever completely mastered, for a singer comes back to it from time to time with her ears making new demands upon her voice and her body, and

thus she must restudy the exercises. Also, singing is such a complicated overlapping of effects that it is necessary to advance in many directions at once in order to make obvious progress. The mere doing of an exercise will accomplish nothing if it is not done with some technical and tonal insight. The following exercises deal with more than one function, and become increasingly complicated.

EXERCISE 1

Swallow air into a throat that is as relaxed as possible—a yawn position of the throat is appropriate. Let the air out slowly on a "ssss" and be aware of what is happening to the rib cage. Correct your posture, maintaining a high chest position without a tense or high shoulder position. Take another breath without moving the chest, let out slowly on a "ssss," and this time watch your rib cage, specifically to keep it from falling. It should not be any higher at the end of the expiration than it was before you took your breath, or any lower. If it is, take note of the position of your rib cage *before* you take the next breath. If it is artificially high (that is, held up by shoulder muscles) before you take a breath, you will have to let it drop as the breath leaves your body. Then, with the next breath you will find yourself in the position of blowing up your body with your breath in much the same manner as you blow up a balloon. No singer has the time or energy to spend on a process such as that, and therefore the body must assume an easy stance before the breathing process begins and maintain it throughout. Begin the process again, placing your hands so that the little fingers rest at the sides of the waist and toward the back, and so that the thumbs reach toward the lowest two ribs. Take a breath. Feel the expansion and press out slightly with these muscles as the air goes out. Keep the rib cage at the proper level. Practice before a mirror. The minute you run out of breath or find yourself gasping for a breath with the upper chest in motion, go back to the beginning and start all over again.

This exercise should help you to develop the habit of using the right breathing muscles, with the place of expansion between your waist and the lower two ribs. The exercise should not be forgotten, for after illness, or as the body matures, or during a bout of nerves, it will be necessary to recheck the procedure.

EXERCISE 2

Sigh. Sigh again, this time making sure that the motion starts with a decided muscular action just below your waistband. This action should push in in order to push the air out. There should be absolutely no tension at the throat level. There should be no feeling of "making" sound at the level of the larynx. Sigh on a tone in the middle of your range. Make sure the rib cage is in the proper position. Hold the note, propelling the tone from the abdominal muscles without tightening the jaw. Sigh into an exercise of three notes, up and then down. Hold the last note, and be aware of a slight muscular push near the middle of the abdominal cavity while the rib cage remains high.

Pant. Try to pant with loose short motions with your lower abdominal muscles. Keep the shoulders loose and down. Sing a fast scale with this panting motion. Do not use too much air on the panting, but try for short breaths much like those used by a hot puppy.

EXERCISE 3

Sing a note on the high side of your range (above F for high voices, above D for low voices). Slowly sing a portamento down the octave. Try to keep the sound at the same "bright" forward place in your mouth on the low notes that it occupied on the high ones. Try the vowels [ae] and [ɛ]. Pout your lips slightly, and let the under side of your upper lip assume a slight outward and upward movement. Check the placement of your head and jaw. Has the jaw wandered out as well as down? Strive for a downward motion only. Sigh onto a tone and pronounce the vowels [a]-[e[-[i]-[o]-[u]. The tongue should remain in a loose position throughout. Watch in a mirror and try to keep the tension out of the tongue on the vowels [e]-[i]. Match the position of the tongue on these difficult vowels to the relaxed feeling between the back teeth that you find on other vowels. Go directly from this loose position on the [a] sound to the [i] sound and back again while you watch in the mirror. Now listen to the resulting sound. Learn to hear undue tension on vowels and to correct the sound instantly.

EXERCISE 4

(In general: female high voices begin the ascending exercises on the E above middle C, male high voices on the octave below, low voices on middle C, and baritones on the octave below, and work upward.)

This exercise will help measure the amount of breath at your command while concentrating on the tone quality and the posture needed to produce proper tone. A normal intensity is required. The exercise is to be sung on one breath: stop when the breath runs out, and start again. The exercise is useless if done in falsetto or crooned. The beginning student will use the steps merely to measure breath capacity. The intermediate student will use it as a device to match vocal tones. The advanced student will discover that his breath does not last as long as it did when he first started, but that his tone is more consistent and full. *Be sure that your posture is correct before taking a breath and that you take the breath with an open throat.*

EXERCISE 5

High voices start this exercise on high G, low voices on D, medium voices on E. Slowly sing the scale downward with a break and a breath at *sol.*

This breath should be a long and relaxed one. Repeat *sol* and finish the scale. Make sure that each tone is matched to the one above it. The tone quality should be neither hooty nor raspy.

EXERCISE 6

Use a note in the lower part of your voice. Sigh into the note and portamento slowly up the octave and back down again. Hold the final note and listen to it carefully. If it sounds different from the first note of the exercise, the last sound is probably more correct. Try the exercise again and see if the first note can be corrected.

Reverse the procedure. Start on a note above F for high voices, D for low. Slide down and then up, and listen for the final tone.

Exercises 1–6 have obviously mixed two functions: breathing and phonation—that is, the energy behind the sound and the placement of the sound. Concentration on the phonation and resonation of sound now continues.

EXERCISE 7

Sigh a note in the comfortable part of your voice. Check posture and breath. If you have already discovered that there is a "floating" feeling connected with a well-supported tone, you will at least know when you are correct. Permit a slight motion in the upper abdominal region to make a change in the flow of air (the inward motion of a pant will do). Do not permit your throat to make this change. Hold the note steady, bring in the corners of the lips *slightly*, and maintain a slight outward, upward motion with the upper lip. Do not move the jaw, just the upper lip. Make sure there is no tension at the back of the tongue. The sound [wa] is made with a forceful motion of the lips, not the tongue or the jaw. Try this sound for each note of the following exercise. Then try [we]. Experiment to see if you can feel and hear the difference between a sound produced with lip participation and a sound produced with lazy lips. Do the same exercise on a *sa*. Use a quick abdominal muscle movement coupled with a sharp *s* sound produced by the tip of the tongue in the front center of the mouth.

[sa]
[wa]
[ta]

EXERCISE 8

This exercise is an attempt to coordinate the quick, energetic action of the upper abdominal muscles, a loose tongue, and diction. Use only the tip of the tongue to produce consonants. Repeat the entire exercise progressively faster, grouping three and four repetitions in one breath. If the tongue is tense, it will be impossible to sing very many groups through. Check the breathing muscles and the abdominal muscles to make sure they are doing their share of the work, and attempt to relax the throat and shoulder muscles.

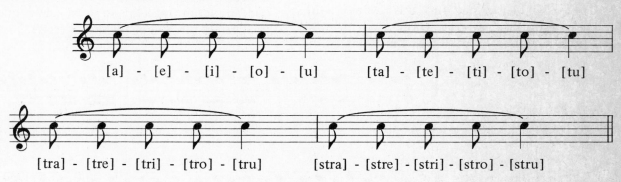

[a] - [e] - [i] - [o] - [u]   [ta] - [te] - [ti] - [to] - [tu]

[tra] - [tre] - [tri] - [tro] - [tru]   [stra] - [stre] - [stri] - [stro] - [stru]

EXERCISE 9

This exercise furthers the coordination of muscles and sound. Short sounds are used, and the beginning of each note as well as the ending of the final note is accompanied with vitality in the abdominal muscles. The sound *m* is made with the lips, and *l* is produced in the same manner as *t*—that is, with the tip of the tongue doing the traveling and not the jaw. Return to exercise 8 and substitute *l* for *t*. Reverse the consonant and vowels to an arrangement of [al]-[el]-[il]-[ol]-[ul]. Remain on the vowel sound until the very last moment. Do not permit your tongue to crawl upward into the consonant while you are holding the vowel. The consonants [n], [m], [l], and [r] are particularly nasty in this respect. Do not anticipate these consonants. *Tones are sung on vowel sound. They are interrupted for very short but precise consonants. Any interruption of the vowel sound will distort the basic vocal sound. Diction makes such distortion necessary, and consonants must therefore be short and energetic.*

[ma] - [mi] - [mu] - [la]

EXERCISE 10

This is an exercise for agility. Tone quality should be consistent and light throughout. It will be advantageous to try many different vowel sounds for the exercise and determine which one works best, and at what range for your voice. Repeat the exercise throughout your range.

Beginners should not feel that they must get through the whole exercise without a breath. It is better to breathe than to be tied up in knots.

[ɛ]
[i]
[a]

EXERCISE 11

Advanced students may find this exercise helpful in learning how to trill. Those students who have trouble rolling r's may find that their trill is long in coming. A tight tongue may do many things; as far as the singer is concerned, they are all bad. Sometimes it helps to use a giggle tone to find the correct placement for this exercise.

EXERCISE 12

Male singers begin a scale passage in falsetto. Carefully assume a proper mouth position, a position where there is some muscle activity in the lips. Come down the scale, allowing the natural voice to appear where it will.

Female voices start on a pitch below fourth-space E and sing down the scale until they reach the end of their range. At this point start a new scale upwards, trying to achieve enough of the lighter characteristics of the voice without losing the warmth of the heavy adjustments, so that the tone will remain consistent.

The sound from exercise 12—particularly the "chest" or lower-adjustment voice of the woman—ought to be checked frequently by a voice teacher. Above all there should be no pushing of this tone. Extended practice of either exercise for either male or female without the help of a voice teacher's ears is not recommended. *Important:* As exercises are practiced there should come a time when suf-

ficient body responses are in balance so that the singer feels an adjustment in the placement of her breathing for the more difficult notes at the high and low parts of her range, as well as for some of the more difficult vowels on any given note. In general, granted the feeling of a circle parallel to the floor that for a normal singing tone appears to be at the bottom of the rib-cage floor, the circle will appear to rise for lower tones. The circle has a *slight* tension outwards at its rim.

EXERCISE 13 *(Messa di Voce)*

A *messa di voce* starts softly (sliding from the high frontal resonance) on any given pitch, increases dynamically, and returns to the soft sound. There should be no "bump" between the soft and louder portions of the sound. It may be increased to two complete cycles —soft-loud-soft-loud-soft—as breath control increases. It is best to begin at the upper-middle section of your range, securely starting the sound in the high placement, and come down note by note. When singing, all high notes start softly. *Messa di voce* is a good way to practice this technique. Exercise 17 can be incorporated with this technique to good advantage.

There are a few places and a few times at which dogmatic statements are valid. This is one of them. All voices—light, heavy, high, or low—should be capable of moving lightly and evenly over their entire range, and of performing proficient runs, jumps, and ornaments that do not destroy the rhythm of the music, change the basic sound of the voice as far as the listener is concerned, or sound labored. One cannot expect the same range or degree of coloratura ability from all voices, but all singers should have the technique to hear and to feel the sound that is appropriate to their voices.

This sound should be on the light side of any particular voice. That is, the thin adjustment and a good deal of the high frontal placement should be used for the total sound. It should be brilliant without being piercing, and it should be consistent from one end of the range to the other. If the sound is a piercing one, the singer should check the width and shape of his pharyngeal cavity. By experimentation and with the help of another pair of ears (a teacher's), the singer can find sound that is ringing without being piercing in quality.

A session of diligent listening to those voices noted for their coloratura work will suggest that singers do not necessarily use the same vowel during coloratura passages. They are apt to change the vowel sound in order to maintain the same vocal sound throughout the runs, frequently using bright sounds. The vowel sounds range from dark to bright:

$$[i]-[e]-[E]-[a]-[ae]-[o]-[u]$$
bright⟵⟶dark

It is a good idea not to consider the schwa sound [ə] or an [ʌ], for they are not easy to hold with enough character to help in the definition of coloratura. The sounds [ɛ], [i], and [ae] are helpful in coloratura singing.

In general, it is necessary to change the vowel sound toward the brighter end of the spectrum as the voice goes downward. Moreover, higher support is needed from the rib cage, with an increasing feeling of body lift as the pitch descends, for the notes below the middle of the range. Thus, the sound will be more focused at the bottom end of the singing range, and it is easier on these vowels to maintain a light sound in the lower voice.

The dark vowels are more difficult to move, mainly because they are back in the throat where it is difficult to carry them or to move quickly. The simple addition of an umlaut sound to an [u] will help immensely, generally allowing the text, if any, to be understood. In general, however, most highly florid passages have texts that are merely being repeated, and the audience already understands thoroughly what is being said. Aside from this, the habit of the human ear to hear what it expects to hear is rather well documented.[1] Consequently, audiences understand a coloratura's shifting vowels. These vowels make the runs more brilliant.

American singers with American speech habits can easily turn alleluia [ae-lɛ-lu-ja] into [a-le-lu-ja]. An early sixteenth century treatise suggests that roulades should be sung on [i] or [e] rather than on the dark [a] [o] [u].[2] Since the gentleman was talking about Latin singing, one can assume that alleluia would not have any of its ornamental work done on an [a] vowel but rather on a vowel modified toward the brighter [i] or [e].

Experimentation with voices and students has produced the following thoughts on the choice of vowel for the most efficient movement in terms of speed and resonance in the medium range.

[1]See, for example, Pierre Delattre's work on consonant clues in "The Physical Atributes of Speech," *Eric*, No. 010231, pp. 61-82.

[2]Georg Quitschreiber, De Canendi Elegantia, Octodecim praecepta, Musicae studiosis necesssaria, Thurston, Dart; trans. cited by Dart in "How they Sang in Jena in 1598, *The Musical Times*, 108, (April 1967), 316.

1. It will vary from student to student.
2. It will vary with the student's maturity and insight.
3. Students whose placement is easily forward and whose sensation of resonance is fairly well established generally produce a good [ɛ] sound.
4. Most Americans produce an [ɛ] vowel that is more pointed throughout the range, less diffuse, more easily heard and retained, and less apt to be breathy in mid-voice.
5. Many Americans' speech patterns produce an [o] sound that is too dark to be agile. These singers *do not hear* their own distortion of the vowel, and it is best to discard it until aural maturity is developed.

6. Pronunciation of any vowel sound, as everything else in singing, depends very much upon the breath mechanism.

7. There are times when the demands of coloratura vocalizations finally make students realize the necessity for more and better breathing technique. It sometimes behooves a teacher, therefore, to start these exercises *before* she feels a singer is ready for them (one can always retreat).

Exercises grow with students. The better able they are to perform them the more they will hear what needs to be improved.

EXERCISE 14

A good voice is agile, and is even from top to bottom. That means that a voice should be able to encompass all of the notes within its range, quickly and with fundamentally the same sound. The remainder of the exercises in this section can be of value to you *if* you listen to the sound you are producing, and *if* you train your ear to accept only the sound that is capable of being agile without changing its fundamental tone color.

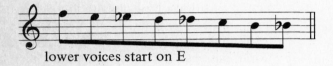

lower voices start on E

EXERCISE 15

All exercises may be repeated on any pitch. This exercise will help you develop rhythmic accuracy plus agility. It may be done in reverse—that is, starting on a low note and singing doublets up the scale. It is necessary in developing rhythmic and vocal accuracy to make sure that both of the doublets are equal in time value, and that the first note is not held longer or shorter than the second.

lower voices start on E

EXERCISE 16

In dealing with triplets you must make sure that the middle note is not slighted. Sometimes it is good to deliberately distort the time values, singing the rhythms ♪♪♪ and then ♪♪♪. After you have done this a few times, restore the correct triplet value and hear the difference.

lower voices start on E

EXERCISE 17

This exercise is helpful for singing notes with definition. It is also helpful for learning how to bring down the sound of the top voice into the bottom voice. Study it from different pitches as written—that is, from the top down. Later, when you feel secure in the sound of the top part of your voice you may reverse it and try it from the bottom up.

EXERCISE 18

This is a difficult exercise. The idea is to make the lower notes sound as though they belong to the same voice that is singing the upper notes.

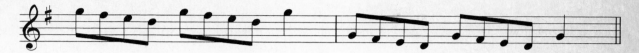

EXERCISES 19–35

The following exercises are taken from the literature. They are written for a particular voice. Remember that sound, particularly at the beginning of a practice session, should be placed in a strong rhythmical frame. Rhythm, when used forcefully and at a good pace, will help the body achieve the muscle agility needed for good tone. When an exercise is learned well, it may be sung in a more subtle ryhthmic fashion.

Exercises for Soprano
Exercise 19: **Lucrezia**

G. F. Handel

German Handel Society edition, vol. 50 (Leipzig, 1887), p. 37, mm. 36-54.

Exercise 20: Lucrezia

G. F. Handel

Furioso

Ques-ti la di - spe - ra - - - - -
Now I shall change des - per - - - - -

- - - ta a - ni-ma mi - a
a - tion to re - venge

German Handel Society edition, p. 38, mm. 1-6.

Exercise 21: Lucrezia

G. F. Handel

Larghetto

Al - la sal-ma in - fe - del por - ga la pe - - - -
to the trai - tor I shall car - ry my re - - - -

- - - - - - na
- - - - - *venge*

German Handel Society edition, p. 40, mm. 1-10.

Exercises for Alto

Exercise 22: Schau, lieber Gott, wie meine Feind *(Cantata 153)*

J. S. Bach

mit e - wi - gen Freu - - - -
with e - ter - nal plea - - - -

- - - - -

den

sure

Bach Gesellschaft edition, Vol. 32, p. 57, mm. 1-13.

Exercise 23: **Samson**

G. F. Handel

no more

German Handel Society edition, p. 91, mm. 16-18.

Exercise 24: **Samson**

G. F. Handel

of earth-ly joys

German Handel Society edition, p. 92, mm. 6-10.

Exercise 25: **Samson**

G. F. Handel

shall then o'er - take

them

German Handel Society edition, p. 93, mm. 13-23.

Exercises for Tenor

Exercise 26: **Lobe den Herrn, Meine Seele** *(Cantata 143)*

Je - su, Ret - ter, dei - ner Her - de, blei-be fer - ner un - ser hort.

Je - sus, Sav - ior, of your peo-ple stay for-ev - er as our guide.

Bach Gesellschaft edition, Vol. 30, p. 62-63, mm. 3-7.

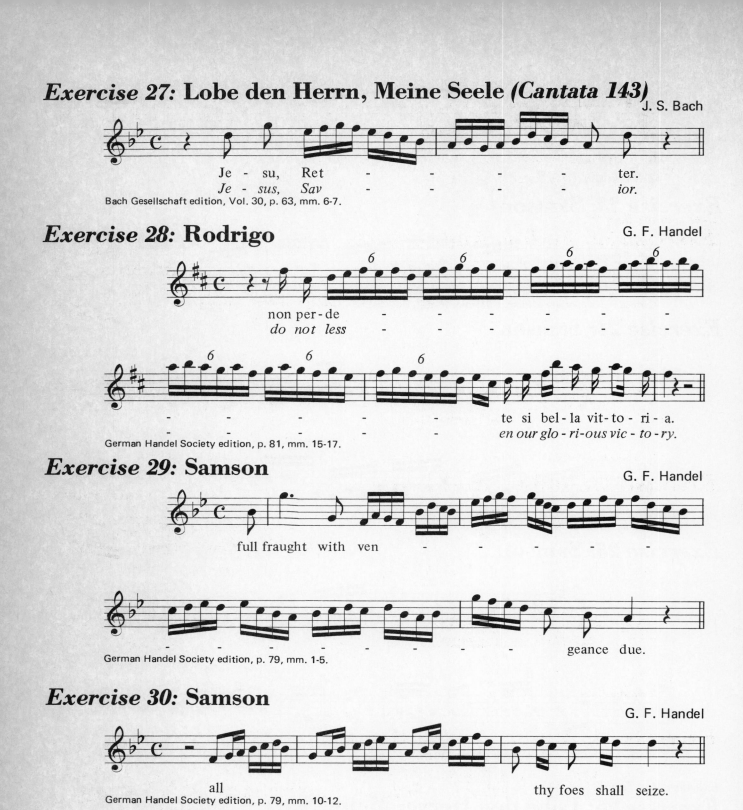

Exercise 27: Lobe den Herrn, Meine Seele *(Cantata 143)*

J. S. Bach

Je - su, Ret - - - - - ter.
Je - sus, Sav - - - - - ior.

Bach Gesellschaft edition, Vol. 30, p. 63, mm. 6-7.

Exercise 28: Rodrigo

G. F. Handel

non per - de - - - - -
do not less - - - - -

\- - - - - te si bel - la vit - to - ri - a.
\- - - - - *en our glo - ri - ous vic - to - ry.*

German Handel Society edition, p. 81, mm. 15-17.

Exercise 29: Samson

G. F. Handel

full fraught with ven - - - - -

\- - - - - - geance due.

German Handel Society edition, p. 79, mm. 1-5.

Exercise 30: Samson

G. F. Handel

all   thy foes shall seize.

German Handel Society edition, p. 79, mm. 10-12.

Exercise 31: Samson

G. F. Handel

may hear how we re - joice - - - -

German Handel Society edition, p. 30, mm. 10-14.

Exercises for Bass

Exercise 32: **Audite, Audite Regis**

G. B. Bassani

Cae - lum ap - pe   ru it

Heav - en con - sum   *ing us*

Harmonia Festiva (London: William Pearson for John Cullen and John Young, 1708), pp. 70-71, mm. 15-17.

Exercise 33: **Audite, Audite Regis**

G. B. Bassani

poe - nes de - co - ran   ter.

Sal - va - tion to our hon   *or.*

Harmonia Festiva, p. 71, mm. 29-32.

Exercise 34: **Audite, Audite Regis**

G. B. Bassani

al-le-lu-ia   al - le - lu - ia

Harmonia Festiva, p. 83, mm. 11-16.

Exercise 35: Lobe den Herrn, Meine Seele *(Cantata 143)*

J. S. Bach

der Herr ist Kö - nig e - - - - -
The Lord is King e - ter - - - - -

- - - - wig - lich
- - - - *nal - ly*

Bach Gesellschaft edition, Vol. 30, pp. 59-60, mm. 10-19.

chapter iv

Songs and How to Sing Them

The songs in this chapter are also exercises. They are not to be sung with accompaniment, and have been selected for that reason. It is necessary for beginning voice students to hear their own tone quality, and it is all too easy for them to lose their ear for the singing tone in an attempt to blend into the piano part. Many beginning students are so concerned with the correctness of musical performance that they never learn to listen to their own voices. These songs were selected because they "make sense" without accompaniment and are more apt to force singers to listen to their vocal tone.

TO FIND A BASIC VOCAL SOUND

Singers, like other musicians, must find out how a phrase should sound from the inside of the music. It is the sound they should be concerned with primarily. They must be able to recognize their basic sound, and to use this basic sound in order to produce a basic musical line. The line is musical and really cannot be described accurately in words. Sometimes it is of value to note that within the basic musical line one note begins in intensity and color precisely where the last note left off. Generally speaking, this musical concept of line, tone, and color can be presented only in sound itself. Therefore, these rather simple songs are offered as beginning studies with some musical challenge that students may use to try to form a concept of tone, line, and color. Students should not try for dramatic or comic effects, for additional coloring, for too many crescendos and ritards, or for the use of soft voice *until* they have achieved a basic line and a basic tone quality for their voices. Within the con-

text of basic vocal quality they can distort color and phrase as they like and still produce a genuinely musical sound.

One word of caution. All vocal students must have a minimum voice. Not just the minimum excellence of performance that they must maintain, in spite of sickness, disaster, or an attack of the "blahs," if they are to be professional; that is essential also. There must also be, in terms of dynamic level, a minimum sound. If they go below that minimum (something that can occur easily with a very sensitive student trying to be artistic), the voice will not carry, and will lose its basic characteristic. An exercise in *messa di voce* (see exercise 13 in the preceding chapter) is a fairly accurate way of gaining some indication of the range of dynamics of a specific voice. But total indications change from room to room, from altitude to altitude, and sometimes from Tuesday to Tuesday. Advanced students and professionals frequently need to be told when they have produced a sound below the minimum. Unfortunately, the sound in this bracket may be a perfectly acceptable sound—to them, not to the audience.

ANTICIPATING TROUBLE SPOTS

All pieces of music are essentially exercises. Troublesome spots should be taken out of context, analyzed, and practiced until conquered. Students all have their peculiarities, their own brand of mistakes, but some mistakes are made over and over. In an effort to recognize these, consider the following possibilities.

High notes are usually missed because a preceding low note in the phrase was not placed "forward" enough (in the lift position), and the shifting of gears became impossible.

A phrase containing a high note and a low note can be kept at the same level only if one remembers that in the nature of things the higher note will sound louder and more brilliant than the lower note. It is up to the singer to make the difference as slight as possible.

Take a breath at the expense of the note you are leaving. Always begin each new phrase at the exact time indicated.

In strophic music, and in musical forms where a section is repeated several times (a rondo, for instance), note that ritards must not be taken at the end of each strophe or each presentation of the repeated section. Rhythm must be maintained, and if a ritard is in order, the rhythm must be immediately reestablished (church hymn directors, take note).

Exact repetition of words and music requires a change in dynamics or in phrasing.

Consonants must be sharp and quick, with no anticipation that might allow the tongue to tighten.

Phrases including rests as part of a dramatic effect should not be chopped up with breathing.

Rests are merely not sung, but the phrase includes silence as an entity. Technically you can accomplish this by continuing to sing in your mind, and by establishing the same dynamic level for the note after the break that you used for the note prior to it.

If the rib cage is held up throughout the cycle of breathing, it becomes possible to snatch an inaudible small breath, particularly as a part of the pronunciation of beginning consonants. The audience will not hear an audible gasp, and will be none the wiser. With a small lift of the soft palate, just enough to realign the head and neck, the singer can obtain enough spare breath to finish a phrase easily. In particularly long passages the singer can accomplish a number of these small breaths, which can provide more fuel for the phrase than a large gasp. In long coloratura passages, jumps of a fourth, fifth, or octave—particularly upward jumps—frequently provide substantial time for a short lift. (In the singing of Baroque music, the upward jump of the fourth and fifth often demands stylistic treatment similar to the lift. This is of some advantage to singers trying to negotiate the long florid passages in Bach or Handel, for instance.)

SONGS WITHOUT ACCOMPANIMENT

Name	*Aim*
Brothers Come	Simple phrasing
What Grows up in the Hills	Diction at a fast tempo
You Golden Sunshine	Line; stepwise motion; long phrases
It Is a Lovely Heavenly Place	Line; negotiation of fast, light values
Lord, Oh Spare Me	Line; consistent tone quality
Black Is the Color	Line; complicated rhythms
Tune Thy Music to Thy Heart	Line; diction without destroying the line; negotiating overbar scansion
Maids Are Simple	Performance of a comic song
Could My Heart	Long sustained line
Weep You No More	Difficult rhythm; sustained line

Some of the following songs are canons. They will allow students to hear part music and combinations of vocal sounds. Equal voices give opportunities for many combinations.

The Snow Will Go	Canon
Laugh Canon	Canon; use of fast downward runs
Miserere	Canon; slow line
Yes and No	Canon; rhythmic problems and comic-performance possibilities
Go Tell It on the Mountain	Spirited solo number
Over Yandro	Solo material for low voices

Heaven's Stars	Difficult phrasing
Sometimes I Feel	Heartfelt music for perfomance practice
An die Musik (To Music)	Both the English and German words are given. Once mastered, find the original accompaniment composed by Schubert and see how vocal line and piano fit together.

Brothers Come

Folk Song

Broth-ers come_ now join_ in drink-ing, Praise_ the

an - cient fa-ther of think - ing. Emp - ty the glass - es,

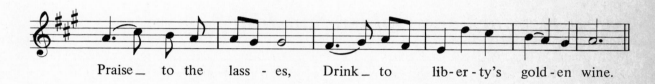

Praise_ to the lass - es, Drink_ to lib-er-ty's gold -en wine.

What Grows Up in the Hills

Folk Song

What grows up in the hills, what grows up in the

hills, what grows up in the steep ston - ey hills,

yes, yes, steep ston - ey hills, what grows up in the hills?

You Golden Sunshine

J. S. Bach

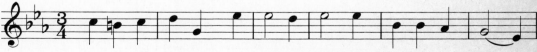

You gold-en sun-shine, oh joy-ful life - line, cov - er my hours_

with your warm show-ers, with your heart quick-en-ing, love-ly light.

I met each mor-row with dark-est sor-row, now I shall stand high, let

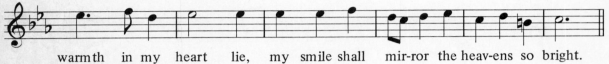

warmth in my heart lie, my smile shall mir-ror the heav-ens so bright.

Schemell; Gesangbuch, No. 13.

Lower Key for "You Golden Sunshine"

You gold-en sun-shine, oh joy-ful life-line, cov-er my hours

with your warm show-ers, with your heart quick-en-ing, love-ly light.

I met each mor-row with dark-est sor-row, now I shall stand high, let

warmth in my heart lie, my smile shall mir-ror the heav-ens so bright.

It Is a Lovely Heavenly Place

F. Schubert

It is a love-ly heav-en-ly place this par-a-dise of

charm-ing lace where earth is cov-er'd with flow-ers and where the birds with

sil-ver bells be-side the streams do chant their spells from

bud-ding spring-time bow-ers and where the birds with sil-ver bells be-

side the streams do chant their spells from bud-ding spring-time bow-ers.

Blumenlied (Frankfort: C. F. Peters), Vol. VII, pp. 100-101.

Lower Key for "It Is a Lovely Heavenly Place"

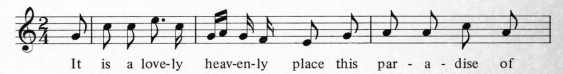

It is a love-ly heav-en-ly place this par-a-dise of

charm-ing lace where earth is cov-er'd with flow-ers and where the bids with

sil-ver bells be-side the streams do chant their spells from

bud-ding spring-time bow-ers and where the birds with sil-ver bells be-

side the streams do chant their spells from bud-ding spring-time bow-ers.

Lord, Oh Spare Me

J. S. Bach

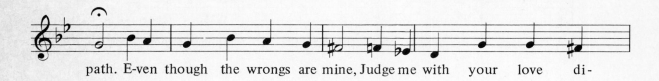

Lord, oh spare me from_ your wrath. For the e-vil grown in my

path. E-ven though the wrongs are mine, Judge me with your love di-

vine. Free-ly I ad-mit my fall - ing, And my soul to Thee is call-

ing. Now oh Lord, up-on Thy throne, lov-ing Fa - ther judge Thy own.

Schemelli Gesangbuch, No. 27.

Black Is the Color

Folk Song

Black, black, black is the col-or of my true love's hair, {her} {his}

lips are some-thing ros - y fair._ The pert-est face and the

{dain - ti - est} {strong - est} hands, I love the grass where-on {she} {he} stands._

Tune Thy Music to Thy Heart

Thomas Campion

Tune thy mu - sic to thy heart; sing thy joy with
Love can won-drous things ef - fect; sweet - est sac - ri -

thanks, and so thy sor - row, though de - vo - tion needs not art,
fice, and wrath ap - peas - ing, love the high-est doth re - spect,

some - times of the poor the rich may bor - row.
love a - lone to him is ev - er pleas - ing.

Edmund Horace Fellowes, ed., *English School of Lutenist Song Writers* (London: Stainer & Bell), Vol. 1, p. 12, vv. 1, 3.

Maids Are Simple

Thomas Campion

Maids are sim - ple, some men say. They for-sooth will trust no men.
Love a make a pure blind child. But let none trust such as he.

But should they man's wills o - bey Maids were ver - y sim-ple then.
Rath - er than to be be - guiled Ev - er let me sim-ple be.

Lutenist Song Writers, Vol. 10, p. 8.

Could My Heart

Thomas Campion

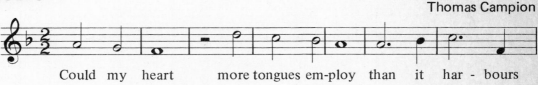

Could my heart more tongues em-ploy than it har - bours

thoughts of grief; it is now so far from joy

that it scarce could ask re - lief. Tru - est hearts _____ by

deeds un - kind to de - spair are most in - clined.

Lutenist Song Writers, Vol. 10, p. 44.

Weep No More

John Dowland

Weep_ you no more, sad foun-tains; What need you flow so
Sleep_ is a re - con - cil - ing. A rest that peace be -

fast? Look_ how the snow-y moun-tains Heav'ns sun doth gen - tly
gets. Doth_ not the sun-rise smil - ing When fair at e'en it

waste, But my sun's_ heav-en - ly eyes. View not your
sets. Rest you then _____ rest _____ sad eyes. Melt not in

weep - ing that now lies sleep - ing, that now lies sleep - ing,
weep - ing while she lies sleep - ing, while she lies sleep - ing,

soft - ly, soft - ly now soft - ly lies _____ sleep - ing.
soft - ly, soft - ly now soft - ly lies _____ sleep - ing.

Lutenist Song Writers, Vol. 10, p. 58.

The Snow Will Go

Franz Schubert

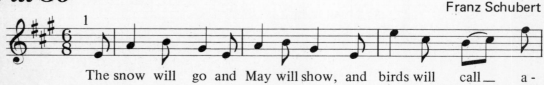

The snow will go and May will show, and birds will call_ a -

round us all. Who knows how soon we'll hear their tune, who

knows how soon we'll hear their tune? The sun's warm light will

shine so bright, en - joy the sun, God's will be done.

Fritz Jöde, ed., *Der Kanon*. (Wolfenbüttel: Möseler Verlag), Vol. III, p. 14.

Laugh Canon

Friedrich Kuhlau

Ha, ha, ha, ha, ha, ha, ha, ha, ha! Hail the man, who finds

laugh-ter when e'er he can, who finds laugh-ter, finds laugh-ter when e'er he

can. Lone his pain and cold his sor-row, but with joy he laughs to-

mor-row, but with joy he laughs to - mor - row, for___ who dares to

laugh and grin will find all___ the world will love him.

Der Kanon, Vol. II, p. 62.

Miserere

Adam Gumpelzhaimer

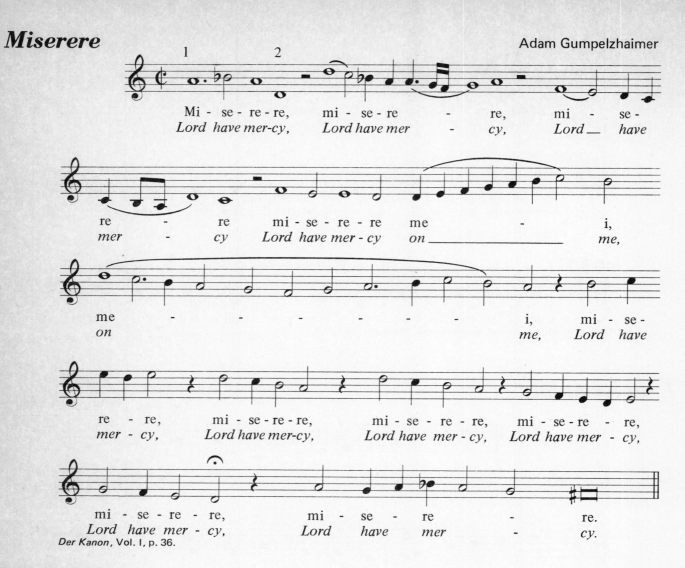

Mi - se - re - re, mi - se - re - re, mi - se -
Lord have mer-cy, Lord have mer - cy, Lord — have

re - re mi - se - re - re me - i,
mer - cy Lord have mer - cy on ___ me,

me - i, mi - se -
on me, Lord have

re - re, mi - se - re - re, mi - se - re - re, mi - se - re - re,
mer - cy, Lord have mer-cy, Lord have mer - cy, Lord have mer - cy,

mi - se - re - re, mi - se - re - re.
Lord have mer - cy, Lord have mer - cy.

Der Kanon, Vol. I, p. 36.

Yes and No

Franz Joseph Haydn

Her glance says yes, her glance does, Her mouth al - ways says

no yes no. No one can ev - er tell what wom-en

mean, or so it seems, or so it seems, it seems.

Der Kanon, Vol. II, p. 21.

Go Tell It on the Mountain

Folk Song

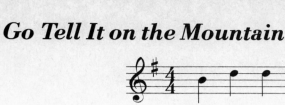

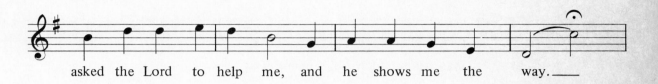

When I was a seek-er I sought both night and day. I

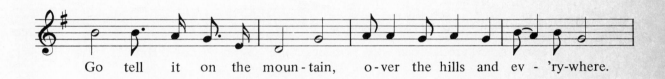

asked the Lord to help me, and he shows me the way.___

Go tell it on the moun-tain, o-ver the hills and ev-'ry-where.

Go tell it on the moun-tain, our heav'n-ly Lord___ is born.

Over Yandro

Folk Song

I'm goin' a-way for to stay a lit-tle while. But I'm

com-ing back, if I go ten thou-sand miles. Oh, who will tie

your shoes? And who will glove your hand? And who will kiss those ru-by

lips when I am gone? Look a-way, look a-way o-ver Yan-dro.

Olin Downes and Elie Siegmeister, *A Treasury of American Songs* (New York: Knopf, 1943), p. 222. Copyright 1940, 1943. Reprinted by permission of Elie Siegmeister.

Heaven's Stars

J. S. Bach

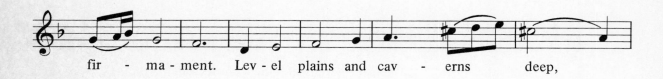

Heav-en's stars, you winds that leap, and you bril - liant

fir - ma - ment. Lev - el plains and cav - erns deep,

rocks_ where_ ech - o's songs_ are sent. Praise Him_ joy - ful - ly,

join our sing - ing till both earth and heav-en are ring - ing.

Schemelli Gesangbuch, no. 40.

Sometimes I Feel

Spiritual

Some-times I feel like a moth-er-less child. Some-times I feel like a

moth - er - less child. Some-times I feel like a moth-er - less child a

long way from home,___ a long way from home. True be-liev-er, a

long way, a long,___ a long way_ from home.

36

An Die Musik (To Music)

Franz Schubert

Du hol-de Kunst in wie viel grau-en Stun-den
You ho-ly art in these deep gray-filled hours

wo mich des le-bens wil-der Kreis um-strickt, Hast du mein
when all my life is bound in wild de-spair you've brought my

Herz_ zu_ war-mer Lieb ent-zun-den hast mich in ei-ne
heart_ the_warmth of love's kind show-ers, and show'd me how a

bess-re Welt ent-rückt, in ei-ne bess-re Welt_ ent-rückt.
bet-ter world can care, show'd me a bet-ter world_ can care.

Schubert Songs (Frankfort: C. F. Peters), Vol. I, p. 236, V. I.

chapter v
Diction

The simplest of the vowel sounds and their International Phonetic Alphabet symbols are listed below. They should be pure; that is, there should be no introduction of another vowel into the initial sound. The greatest number of impurities occur with the sound [e]. In general American speech there exists a slur from the pure [e] into an [i] sound. We frequently close a [g e-i t] when we are [l e-i t]. The temptation to make such a slur at the end of an [e] or an [o] which results in a diphthong, is one that must be eliminated in the pronunciation of Italian, French, and German. It is also a temptation the singer should avoid in singing English, for it provides just enough excuse for the tightening of jaw and tongue to lead to a tight sound.

Basic Vowel Sounds

Spelling	IPA Symbol	Examples
A	[ɑ]	far, alms
	[a]	bath (as pronounced in New England), my [maɪ]
	[ae]	cat
	[ʌ]	above
E	[e]	gate (without diphthong)
	[ɛ]	let
	[ə]	sofa, the (this is called the schwa sound)
I	[i]	machine
	[I]	pity
O	[o]	go
U	[ɔ]	all, taught
	[u]	tooth
	[U]	pull

The phrase "sing on the vowels" is meaningful only if the vowels that one "sings on" are free from tension and pure. Some students find that an effective tool for the examination of the balance of resonance and the breathing apparatus is the study of pure vowels. Such students are able to hear and to feel the differences in sound and formation among the vowels. Other students find different avenues of study more advantageous.

Consonants should be pronounced in a frontal position. This is difficult, for most of our American speech patterns are placed farther back in the mouth. When the tip of the tongue is placed just behind the upper teeth, and the rest of the tongue is kept in a working but relaxed position the resulting consonants will be forward and crisp. Clarity of consonants should not be considered an effect of the length of the consonant, but rather of the crispness. An energetic but quick consonant will not destroy the initial and continuing flow of the vowel sound. Singers must sing on the vowel sound for beautiful tone. On the other hand, the words must be intelligible without affecting the tone. The words, or the consonants that make the words, are necessary noise interrupting the flow of sound. As such they must be short and powerful enough to be understood. Crisp, forward consonants are important.

The handling of consonants that occur after the vowel is difficult for most singers. The consonants *l, m, n,* and *r* are particularly troublesome. These consonants are often anticipated in our speech patterns. For instance, we frequently anticipate the *r* of *hear* at the beginning of the vowel. Anticipation means that the tongue starts its movement toward the placement for the consonant while it should be remaining still for the vowel sound. This has the effect of tightening the tongue and pulling it back at a time when the vowel sound should be pure and unhindered.

Diction is not a function of the tongue, teeth, and lips alone. Proper singing diction also requires diaphragmatic-intercostal breath and support, which enables the singer to use his breath without unnecessary tension in the neck, shoulder, and tongue, particularly the root of the tongue. It will be discovered that the same force used to propel the air upwards—abdominal pressure—can be coupled with the formation of consonants. This muscular action can relieve the base of the tongue from some of the tension required in the making of a consonant, and provide the energy for the consonant. Coupling the action of basic tone production with the creation of certain consonants such as s or l is an excellent exercise in coordination.

Consonants are divided into groups: those made by the tongue, those made by the lips, semi-vowels, explosives, fricatives, and nasal consonants. All of these definitions are premised on how the sound is made physically. Singers must add a further consideration to the formation of both vowels and consonants: they must make sure that *where* includes a frontal location as well as a dynamic and quick sound. Perhaps the hardest chore for American speakers is the rediscovery and use of lip muscles.

Our speech patterns do not include the affirmative action of the lip muscles that good singing demands. The consonants *w* and *v* are particularly smeared in our speech. By starting with a whistle position of the lips, which requires the use of the very forward lip muscles, we can achieve clarity in these consonants.

The following exercise may be of value for hearing and feeling the strength and position of consonants. The first goal is to achieve vowel sounds that are free. It should be noted that vowels by their nature change the shape of the pharyngeal and oral cavities.[1] A great deal of the forward placement essential in making vowel sounds is therefore psychological—a feeling rather than a totally physiological fact. It is a feeling, however, that helps to counteract the backward placement that occurs in our normal speech. Vowel sounds should be practiced in front of a mirror, and the singer should feel their placement. She then should attempt to put all the vowels in a "feeling" of forward placement, a feeling that she most probably has on [i] or [e]. The teacher, however, should check this sound, and also check tension at the back of the tongue on all the vowel sounds. It is a good idea to put a poorly placed vowel next to a vowel that is well placed (or vice versa)—for instance:

[i]-[ae]-[i]

In the following sequence, try to keep the vowels forward. A slight use of the lip muscles will help. The jaw should not contract for the [e] or the [i] sound.

[a]-[e]-[i]-[o]-[u]
sung on one tone

Next, preface each of these vowels, without losing the constant vowel sound, with a [t]. This [t] should be produced by a quick, energetic stroke of the tip of the tongue just behind the upper teeth. The tongue should then return to its normal position behind the lower teeth. A *tr* is added next (as in Chapter III, exercise 8). Those people who have difficulty in rolling the *r* may find this simpler when the *r* is coupled to another consonant, as in *br* or *tr*. In that position the base of the tongue is relieved of some of its tension and the lips help to balance the formation of the consonant.

The next exercise places the consonants after the vowels. There should be absolutely no anticipation before the sound is needed.

[a] ---------------------[t] crisply and quickly
no anticipation

---

[1]De Lattre, Pierre, "Acoustics of Vowels." *Eric*, No. 025182, 1968, p. 42.

SENSIBLE DICTION

Using the lips, particularly the upper lip, with more force and muscle tone will produce an effective sound, not an "affected" one, in a style that does not distort the mouth to the point where the audience is uncomfortably aware of the distortion. Nor does such diction change the basic sound of the dialect needed to complete the style. For instance, to sing country-and-western with a New England accent is absurd. To sing American musical comedy with a British accent is equally absurd.

However, to sing anything in such a way that the words cannot be understood defeats the purpose of song.

The placement of the diction pattern in the mouth need not unduly affect the dialect wanted. Balance is what is needed. If a forward sound is needed to make the music heard, and if a backward vowel sound is needed to portray the character of the dialect, a balance can be struck between the two elements that will permit both diction and dialect to be accomplished.

Here are some guidelines for sensible diction.

1. The *r* may be produced in a forward position behind the teeth, a procedure that does not usually happen in American speech. Such an *r* is not trilled, and need not be sounded as a trilled *r*, but it will carry within the dialect chosen for the song and still be comprehensible. An *r* that is made with the tongue touching immediately behind the upper teeth generally produces the correct sound.

2. It is always necessary to carry the tone on the vowel sound and to produce consonants that are overemphasized with energy but not prolonged in time. Sometimes a slight hesitation can underline a beginning consonant or a particularly important one, or a pause can underline a beginning vowel.

3. Vowels can keep the diphthonged drag that is necessary in country-and-western music, if both vowel sounds in the diphthong are kept forward and the jaw is not allowed to drag backwards during the change from one vowel to another.

Hints For Pronunciation Of Foreign Words

1. In most romance languages a double consonant tends to shorten the preceding vowel.
2. Ending vowels are unstressed, and have a shortened sound.
3. The vowels *e* and *i* change the pronunciation of preceding consonants *c* and *g* in Italian, French, and Spanish.
   Italian: *ci* pronounced [či], *gi* pronounced [ji]
          co pronounced [ko], *go* pronounced [go].
   In order to spell the sound [ki], *h* must be added. For example, *chi* is pronounced [ki].
   In Spanish, *ci* and *ce* become [øi] and [øe] (Castilian) or [si] and [se] (South American).
   These changes are called orthographic changes.
4. In Italian, *s* is sometimes pronounced *z* between two vowels (*uso* is *uzo*). Exceptions: *geloso,*
                                      cosi,
                                      naso,
                                      casa,
                                      cosa
   There are other exceptions.
5. Most ending consonants are not heard in French except *c, r, f, l (careful)*. Exceptions include countless infinitives for the first and second conjugations ending in an unspoken *r*.
   Important exceptions: *le fils* (the son) [fis]
                         hélas (alas)   [elas]
                         le lys (the lily) [lis]
6. Some examples of the aspirate *h* in French (these sounds prevent liaison):
haut (and derivatives)	height
hâte	hurry
hasard	chance
hautbois	oboe
honteaux	ashamed

7. In German, the initial [s] is usually pronounced [z]. And initial [s] plus a consonant becomes [ʃ] or [š̌], as in *sterben*. The prefixes *ge-* and *be-* are not regarded when determining the pronunciation of an initial [s]. The *ss* is a very pronounced and vigorous sound; it is considered a single consonant in German. An *st* at the end of a word is pronounced as in English—for example, *last*.

The vowel and consonant charts that follow are by no means complete. Their aim is to present the sounds most needed by the vocal student in four languages.

IPA Vowels

Spelling	IPA Symbol	English	Italian	French	German
AH	[ɑ]	father	Patria	pas	Vater
	[a]	ask		patte	Shatten
AW	[ɒ]	hot			
	[ɔ]	saw			
U	[ʌ]	up			
	[ə]	the			
A	[ae]	had			
EY	[e]	mate	che	et	ewige
EH	[ɛ]	let	letto	est	endlich
E[1]	[ə]			appurtenance	Erbe
I	[i]	machine	di	si	wir
	[I]	pity			ist
O	[o]	go	lo	au, eau	Wogen
O	[ɔ]	sought	occhi	votre	oft
U	[u]	tooth	luna	doux	du
	[U]	put			und
semi-vowels					
	[j]	yes	ieri	yeux	ja
	[w]	suede	questo	oui	
	[y]			nuit	
diphthongs					
	[aI]	night			
	[eI]	day			
	[ɔI]	toy			
	[au]	out			
	[oU]	no			

vowels not found in English				
[ø]	(tense)	form *e* with lips in *o* position	feu	Höhle
[œ̃]	(lax)	form with lips in relaxed *o* position	heure	können
[y]	(tense)	lips form *u*, front of tongue forms *i*	tu	fühl
[Y]	(lax)	shorter than *y*		Hutte
[ɛ̃]		highest nasal	aim, bien	
[ã]		slightly lower	dans	
[ɔ̃]		middle nasal	mon	
[œ̃]		lowest nasal	un	

[1]In French, Italian, and Spanish, *i* and *e* are considered "weak" vowels. They change the pronunciation of a *c* or a *g* that precedes them.

IPA Consonants

Spelling	IPA Symbol	English	Italian	French	German
B	[b]	bat	bella	belle	bist
C	[k]	cat	caro	car	Kaffe
	[s]	facility		facile (c, ci, ce)	
CH	[c]				ich
	[x]	loch			doch
	[k]		che		
	[tʃ] [č]	church	ciaó		
	[ʃ] [š]	shall	scena	chien	Tasche
D	[d]	do	dormire	deux	das
F	[f]	fire	finta	fils	fuhle
G	[g]	grand	grande	grand	gross
	[dʒ] [ǰ]	generous	giro		
	[ʒ] [ž]	vision		jamais	Journal
	[ʎ]		gli		
H	[h]	here		hais[2] (generally silent)	hier
J	[dʒ] [ǰ]	judge	giro		
K	[k]	kitchen			Kunst
L	[l]	late	la	le	Luft
ll	[ʎ]	William	gli	feuille (exceptions: mille, ville, tranquille)	million
M	[m]	mother	madre	mère	Mutter
N	[n]	no	non	non	nein
NG	[ŋ]	singer	lungo (an approximation)		
GN	[ɲ]	canyon (an approximation)	ogni	ligne	
P	[p]	pale	padre	père	putzen
PF	[pf]				Pfennig
Q	[kw]	quite	questa	quatuor (an exception)	
	[kv]				Quale
	[k]	quai		qui	
R	[r][3]	read	caro	rue	Ruhe
S	[s]	stove	sine	sans	Fassen
	[ʃ] [š]	sheet	scene	chien	Schule
T	[t]	time	tempo	temps	takt
TH	[ð]	then			
	[θ]	thin			
V	[v]	very	volta	ventre	was
	[f]				viel
W	[w]	well		oui	
	[m]	where			
	[v]				was

[2]The *h* is silent in French, but it does affect liaison. The aspirate *h* is indicated in the dictionary by an asterisk (*) or an apostrophe (').

[3]The trilled and rolled *r* of Italian, French, and German diction should be learned by imitation. The singer is advised to make all such trills in the forward part of the mouth. All French *r*'s are frontal and trilled in singing.

IPA Consonants

Spelling	IPA Symbol	English	Italian	French	German
X	[ks]	tax		taxi	
	[gs]			existence	
				(prefix ex + vowel)	
Z	[z]	arose	tesoro	saison	Sonne
	[ts]	(hat_s_)	zio (initial)[4]		Ziel
	[dz] [ž]		zero (derived		
			from Arabic)		
			mezzo		
			(an exception)		

[4]The Italian *z* is pronounced [ts] (1) when followed by *ia, ie,* or *io,* or (2) in the middle of a word. It is [dz] [z] when it occurs (1) in verbs ending in *izzare,* (2) in words derived from Greek, Hebrew, or Arabic, and (3) in general when it appears in the initial position. *Zio* is an exception [tsio], as is *mezzo* [medzo].

SUGGESTIONS FOR FURTHER STUDY

Adler, Kurt, *Phonetics and Diction in Singing.* Minneapolis: University of Minnesota Press, 1965. (This book consists of Chapters 4–8 from Adler's book *The Art of Accompanying and Coaching*).

Cartier, Francis, and Martin Todaro, *The Phonetic Alphabet.* Dubuque, Iowa: William C. Brown, 1971.

Coffin, Berton, Ralph Errole, Werner Singer, and Pierre Delattre, *Phonetic Readings of Songs and Arias.* Boulder, Colo.: Pruett Press, 1964.

Errole, Ralph, *Italian Diction for Singers.* Boulder, Colo.: Pruett Press, 1963.

Marshall, Madeleine, *The Singer's Manual of English Diction.* New York: G. Schirmer, 1953.

Moriarity, John, *Diction.* Boston: E. C. Schirmer, 1975.

Nitze, William A., and Ernerst H. Wilkins, *A Handbook of French Phonetics.* New York: Holt, Rinehart & Winston, 1945.

Sheil, Richard R., *A Manual of Foreign Language Dictions for Singers.* Fredonia, N.Y.: Palladian, 1975.

Uris, Dorothy, *To Sing in English: A Guide to Improved Diction.* New York: Boosey & Hawkes, 1971.

Wangler, Hans-Heinrich, *Instruction in German Pronunciation.* St. Paul: EMC, 1966.

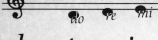

chapter vi

Voice Classification

Voice classification is based on the quality of the voice, the dynamics of the resonating system, and the complicated adjustments of the vocal cords. It has something to do with the range of the voice, but that is not an absolute measure. It has more to do with the quality of the sound.

CHANGES IN REGISTER

Voice teachers use the term *tessitura* when referring to voice classification. The tessitura of the voice is that portion of the range that is the easiest to maintain. Generally, just above this range the voice enters a fourth or fifth of notes that it delivers with a particular shining quality. High voices generally shine from F to high B, and the fifth below the F is fairly easy to maintain in a well trained voice.

In reading about registers one frequently sees the term "break." In high voices, this point is generally given as the F between the shine and the bread-and-butter notes of the singer mentioned above. In medium voices it is E, and low voices D. The set of laryngeal adjustments that are predominant at the lower end of the scale come to an end at about these points, and in order to make sounds above these notes the set of adjustments predominant at the other end of the spectrum must be used. This change is quite noticeable in a raw voice. In a well-developed voice the change will hardly be noticed, for the two sets of adjustments have been so blended that the voice sounds as though it were one continuous chain throughout.

There are a number of different theories concerning these register changes. Some people believe that the voice manifests itself in two distinct forms, one an upper, or head, voice and the other a chest voice. Most of the adherents of this theory realize that the adjustments are actually laryngeal, and that the terms *head* and *chest* are merely helpful, not accurate. Others are convinced that there is only one register. For our purposes let us continue to consider that every note and every dynamic is produced in its own way by the larynx and resonated by the pharyngeal cavities.

VOCAL LIFTS IN THE SCALE

However, we are still faced with the problem of how to classify a voice. The answer is not easy, for the absolute classification of any voice is determined in part by maturity, in part by the quality of the sound, and in part by the training the vocalist has received.

The change notes cited above are sometimes valuable in classifying a voice: F for high, E for middle, and D for low is a pretty good rule of thumb.

However, these "breaks" in the scale are very unreliable in the immature voice or the voice that has been improperly used. Many sopranos, for instance, have a decided change in quality on D because they have never learned to use their lighter adjustment, much less breathe correctly. As they study, this break changes and goes up.

Break is a bad term, for it is negative. The term *lift*, on the other hand, indicates how to overcome these problems in the scale. If the lower tone at a difficult point is approached with the adjustment or the lift indicated for the upper tone, the tones will fall into a scale that sounds unified in tone quality.[1] This means that a soprano heading for a difficult portion of her voice (between D and the third above F) lightens her tone quality without weakening her support, and sings with the feeling of lift so that the scale will adjust to a tone quality that essentially is in line.

There is another trouble point that may affect any voice: the E flat or D above middle C. At this point the resonance provided by the trachea may interfere with voice production. It is often observed that many women have a different sensation on this tone and are tempted into the evils of unsupported chest voice.

None of these points are reliable as a final indication of voice classification, and they are never reliable with the immature student or the student who has not sung correctly. During the first years of teaching, sopraltos and tenitones. abound. It can take several years before a classification can be given to a handful of students. In the meantime they generally wish to sing in ensembles in a medium range. The maturity factor is a sticky one, particularly with the gangling youth. There is no necessity to immediately stick a permanent name on such a voice. Teachers generally get a "feeling" about a voice from its quality, its tessitura, and the body development and the appearance of a student. Even so, mistakes are made and voices must be reclassified from time to time. With maturity, singers get to feel more at ease in one tessitura or another, and will begin to get a "feeling" for where they belong.

The astute teacher will also hear other "breaks" in a voice. For instance, on either third below or above the pivot note there is apt to be another slight change of vocal color—thus the soprano whose high A's are more of a problem than her B flats, or the alto who has a great deal of trouble with the B an octave below. These changes are not always associated with sopranos or altos, for a particular vowel sound, or a particular method of approaching one of these notes, can give any singer a problem. Some rules of thumb can be given: a soprano singing "ah" on the C above middle C usually has more trouble than a mezzo-soprano. Lots of times the high baritone or tenor can have a beautiful middle C and nothing else at the beginning of his studies. But these are all picky issues, and not at all absolute.

[1] Aatto Sonninen, "Paratis-gram of the Vocal Folds and the Dimensions of Voice," *Proceedings of the 4th International Conference of Phonetic Sciences* (Helsinki, 1961), pp. 214-18.

THE IMPORTANCE OF UNDERSTANDING VOWEL FORMATION

Much work has been done recently on the interaction of vowel formation and the fundamental overtones of the pitch being sung.[2] Each vowel is characterized by the dominance of certain frequencies. This configuration is called the formant of the vowel. When one of the formant frequencies matches the frequency of the fundamental or one of the overtones being sung, the pitch is strengthened. For example, the vowel [i] has formants of approximately 400 and 2,100 hertz. A singer singing the G above middle C would have acoustic help from this vowel, since the fundamental of G is 392 hertz (close enough to the 400 of the vowel formant to be helped by it). This information makes it possible to understand that a slight change in the basic sound of the vowel may make a certain note easier to sing, for with every change in the vowel sound there is a shifting of the vowel's formants. This understanding of the basic structure of vowels allows singers to find their best tone on any given pitch by adjusting shadings of a vowel until they have found one that is most suitable for their voices. For information on the frequencies of the tempered scale and on vowel formants see the following tables.

[2]See, for example, Berton Coffin, *The Sounds of Singing* (Boulder, Colo.: Pruett Press, 1977).

Frequencies of the Tempered Scale

Pitch	Fundamental	First overtone
C_6	1,046 hertz[1]	2,093 hertz
B	987	1,975
A	880	1,760
G	784	1,568
F	698	1,396
E	659	1,319
D	587	1,175
C_5	523	1,046
B	493	987
A	440	880
G	392	784
F	349	698
E	329	659
D	293	587
C_4	261	523 (middle C)
B	247	493
A	220	440
G	196	392
F	174	349
E	164	329
D	146	293
C_3	130	261
B	123	247
A	110	220
G	98	196
F	87	174
E	82	164
D	73	146
C_2	65	130

Ranges vary from voice to voice within the same classification. Here are some possibilities:
Soprano
Mezzo-Soprano
Tenor
Baritone
Bass

[1]Figures are rounded.

Vowel Formants

[i]	400 hertz	2,100 hertz
[e]	500	1,800
[ae]	650	1,700
[I]	300	1,500
[ə]	600	1,300
[a]	700	1,100
[u]	450	1,000
[o]	550	900
[ɔ]	650	800

Spoken and sung vowels "drift" quite a bit. The figures above should be considered indications of formant areas. Average vowel formants for females are consistently higher than those for males.

Since the help from any given vowel will be found strongly on one note and probably not on the note either above or below it on the scale, the singer is apt to feel that a new "break" has occurred. This is unfortunate, for it adds to the problems both teacher and singer face in trying to ascertain the correct range for the singer. However, once vowel construction is understood and different vowels and shadings of vowels are carefully used throughout the scale, a pattern will emerge that points to a consistent scale in spite of vowel interference. The effect of the vowel structure on the voice should be remembered when considering the subject of covering to be discussed at the end of this chapter.

COLORATURA REGISTER

The soprano or mezzo-soprano with a high flageolet (flute voice or coloratura register) can present a very disturbing picture to anyone attempting voice classification. Such a singer in an untrained state will frequently have a strong low voice and a very breathy sound in the middle of the range, and then at high C take off into an unusual voice. It takes a great deal of time to train these voices, for their normal singing is quite breathy and most literature written above high C is too difficult for them to sing.

MISCLASSIFICATION

In very large choral groups, singers are often misclassified. There may not be enough time to recheck individuals, but one can check the singers' feelings on the subject! A tense tenor may be a baritone, a bass or a tenor who doesn't know how to use his voice. In large groups it is probably safer to have such men sing the lower part. This is particularly true of high school groups. Many high school tenors find early in their college careers that they are not tenors, and that they have spent a good deal of time practicing the straining of their voices in high school choirs. It is almost impossible for the high school teacher to have sufficient time to correct this evil. If the literature used in the choral work does not demand too high or too low a tessitura, and if the high school teacher does want a warm, unshouted tone quality from his choir, the result will probably not be disastrous. This is equally true of the undergraduate-college choir. It is not good thinking to believe that because your choir can hit all the notes it is all right for them to do so. The tessitura may be too demanding. For instance, most young voices should not be hitting the extremely low notes of Renaissance alto parts. There are very few true alto voices in this world, and they are seldom found in immature singers.

The classification of voices is not an easy thing to do. Voices change with age and training. On the other hand, if sensible ranges and easy tone color are demanded of voices, misclassification is probably not going to be an unforgivable sin. A voice can generally handle a few notes out of its range, as long as it is a *few* notes, as long as they are not yelled, and as long as the singer is diligent in rehearsing the entire range of his or her voice in the practice room. The singers who are waiting patiently to have a final word concerning their classifications can remain waiting patiently. In time they and their teacher will know. Before that time neither will know, and it is better to admit this than to chase after a goal that may be unrealistic.

COVERING AND VOCAL COLOR

As voices approach the top of their range, the part of the larynx that makes the thin adjustment takes over a bigger percentage of the work involved. There ought to be both a feeling of lift at this point and a feeling that the sounds are being covered. An uncovered voice in the high reaches of its range is often uncomfortably brilliant to the listener as well as uncomfortable to the singer.

Covering is a function mainly of vowel modification. How are vowels made? They are made by the adjustment of the cavities of the pharynx and the oral pharynx. This type of adjustment is the same thing that is done in order to give the voice color. The vocal color is darkened by the use of the larger pharynx, or by an [u] sound. The sounds [e] and [I] sound higher to the singer, for their tone has a lighter color. As the singer wishes to enter a covered sound, he attempts a darker sound: [a] goes to [ɔ], [ɛ] goes to [U], and so forth. The quantity and the quality of the sound is a set of concessions that each singer makes with his own voice and diction.

These adjustments can happen fairly naturally in the singer whose jaw and tongue movements are free and who is oriented to the sound of his own voice and the beauty of the music. Such a singer will pull back on the high tones and head for an enlarged area in the back of the pharynx. The larynx will be lower for these high notes, and the back of the throat will feel wider as well as longer. None of these actions will be overdone or pushed. A good singer generally aims for the covered position before it is absolutely necessary. A good singer should also aim to get out of the covered position on the way down in his range. Otherwise, the middle voice and the lower voice will tend to sound hooty or very dull.

chapter vii

Memorization

Memorization is a skill just like any other skill. Just like any other skill it has to be practiced, and just like any other skill some people are more gifted in its activation than others. Why? Heredity or training—probably both. There are individuals with perfect pitch—that is, they have full retention of sound—and there are individuals with perfect visual retention. Most of us do not have to worry about this kind of inheritance, but we do have to worry about improving our ordinary talents to the point where memorization ceases to be a thing of dread, but works for us under stress.

Most of us do not learn logically. Why should we? The child learns to speak in segments, not in logical sentences. We learn to memorize first whatever makes the biggest impression on us. It therefore behooves us to try to make as much of the piece to be memorized fall in that "big-impression" category as soon as possible. It is best to start not with the logical sequence of one measure after another, but by remembering what sticks first and then slowly filling up the holes. Some of us can do this completely by sound, but a far more reliable manner is to memorize both the sound and the look of the page, for the sound can sometimes leave us under stress.

When one is familiar enough with the song so that it has begun to sink in, the process of memorization can begin. There are several steps that may be of value to you.

First of all, know the form; find the repeats. If they are exact, that cuts down on the memorization; if they are not, learn the differences.

Sequences, when they are recognized as such, are fairly simple to memorize.

It is essential to know those spots where the accompaniment and the melody differ.

Do not forget to memorize tempo markings and other written details in the score.

Memorize the length and the sound of the interludes in the accompaniment.

Know the words. Say them apart from the music. Translate foreign words word by word. Understand what the poetry says and what the poetry is trying to convey.

Know the notes. Memorize first the ones that are difficult to sing, and know them by name. "See" the score, and keep building your ability for visual memory.

Develop a feeling for the dramatic side of the song so that the logical sequence of events helps with memorization. Be an actor by memorizing the cause and effect of the meaning of the song as it unfolds in time.

The ear often memorizes before one is conscious of it. Sometimes this is tenuous memory, leaving when one is nervous. Ear memorization is something like a pianist's tactile memorization of the feel of the piano. This type of memorization is good; it needs to be developed more and trusted more. It also needs, for security's sake, to be coupled with visual memorization.

Sing the song silently to yourself. Drill silently. Memorize away from the piano just as you study a score away from the piano. Both skills need to be practiced.

Be patient with yourself. Do not measure your memorization process against anyone else's. Judge it against your own ability. It doesn't matter how long it takes *you* to memorize. It simply has to be done. One will ultimately be graded on the accomplishment; there is no sympathy for the fact that tools such as memorization and vocal technique are more difficult for one person than another.

Only results in the performance field are weighed. Excuses are useless. You either know your stuff and can sell it, or you don't . Either you have your part memorized or you don't, and no one is going to do it for you no matter how glorious your voice is.

Finally, trust your memory. Get away from the music so that you know what it is that you do not know, and so the skills of visual and aural memorization can grow.

As you practice more and more you will discover that sometimes the correct note actually has a feeling to it that helps in the memorization process. We do develop a feeling for the right way of singing a certain vowel on a certain pitch. Unfortunately, this is the first type of memorization to fly out the window at a touch of a cold, during the heightened nerves of a concert, or after a fight with your best friend.

Most of all, don't tell yourself you can't do it. Just *do* it.

chapter viii

Health, Fatigue, and Scheduling

NODES AND OTHER HEALTH PROBLEMS

The nastiest word in the language for a singer is *nodes*. Nodes—the correct term is *vocal nodules*—are a benign thickening of the vocal cords. They may be the result of several different problems that have somehow abused the vocal cords so that they do not strike together correctly. Nodes may be preceded by hemorrhaging at the edge of the cords. Perhaps the single greatest fault leading to a nodule is incorrect speaking. Individuals who speak in a range below their natural speaking level are in trouble. The constant abuse of the cords in this manner—and speaking is more constant than singing—can lead to nodules. Both girls and boys at early ages try to impress their maturity on their audience by assuming unnaturally low voices. Frequently, such abuse follows the speaker into adulthood. Some actors and professional speakers are even trained to assume this range on stage. It is extremely detrimental to vocal health. The same can be said for the unnaturally high voice, but in our society more damage is done by the lowering of the speaking voice to make it sound "sexy" or more "masculine."

Continual exposure of the vocal processes to allergies, asthma, smoking or postnasal drip can also cause an irritation that the cords cannot manage in health. Singers who are always fighting one or another of these irritants may be fighting a losing battle. Of course, individual bodies differ. Some have steel bands for cords, and can take much abuse. Unfortunately, by the time the singer with normal vocal cords has discovered that they cannot take such abuse, it may be too late to rectify the situation. Proper attention to breathing through good singing habits will frequently help the asthma victim.

As for smoking: Don't.

If you must take some form of medication (other than allergy shots) for a medical problem, such as cold or allergy pills, be careful about singing while your throat is dried out from it. It is like running a car with insufficient oil. If the problem is not too serious, allergy medicine can probably be taken at night and that will suffice. Be candid with your doctor when such medicine is prescribed, and discuss fully the ramifications of singing on a dry throat. On the other hand, the constant dripping of allergies can swell the cords, and in time the health problem will become a vocal one. So something does have to be done. If you intend to be a singer, try to get on top of this type of problem quickly so that your health does not detract from your profession. Singing is difficult work and extremely fatiguing for the body. It is not fatiguing for the singing mechanism, however, if the body is doing its work.

FATIGUE

The biggest single killer of young voices is fatigue. During the first hour of rehearsal a determined singer can stay on top of her technique and sing properly. During the second hour fatigue will slowly take over and she will sink into sloppy posture and a tight throat. Singers must remember that their bodies are their instruments; if those instruments are fatigued, they cannot be properly played. This is the damage that overlong rehearsals and overanxious rehearsing can do. It is not the singer's inability to sing that many notes, or that hard; it is the amount of time, and a body that is not well enough coordinated to withstand long rehearsals and their pressures. With experience comes the gradual accrual of endurance.

SCHEDULING

It is right, then, for the student singer to plan ahead. If an opera rehearsal or a set of strenuous choral rehearsals is in the picture for May, any scholastic work that *can* be finished in April ought to be, with ample time left over for sleeping. Procrastination adds extra bookwork and writing time to a schedule already filled with rehearsing. And remember that even though rehearsal time includes a good deal of sitting around and waiting, it is time that is removed from responsibilities and it is tiring time. A singer who puts off until tomorrow what ought to be done before tomorrow's rehearsal will pay dearly for it in body fatigue.

Singing is something that cannot be crammed. It is a physical act and requires daily involvement so that endurance can be built up. One cannot cease singing all week and expect to make it up in one whopping three- or four-hour session on Saturday; the body will rebel. Muscles simply do not work that way. It is best to schedule your singing practice first, and then schedule other activities about it. If you are to be a singer, then the singing should be of prime importance in your scheduling.

ILLNESS

It is not a good idea to sing when you are ill. You will strain your throat trying for something you cannot accomplish because of swelling. Swollen neck glands are extremely difficult to sing with since they throw the whole apparatus out of line. When you are fatigued or ill and must sing, do not sing the extremes of your range. These adjustments of the cords are delicate, and the most difficult to hold correctly. Consequently, they are the first that you will force into the wrong position in order to make them sound at times of stress. Do not sing with a heavy voice, and do sing with as much support as you usually use—and more.

Most important: Do not start to sing with a tight throat and a forced sound. This sound, which is similar to a nasty "ugh" made in the throat, is a glottal attack, and its continual use is *extremely* harmful. Pop singers take note! Try to start each phrase on a sigh. *If* you need to be dramatic, use the consonants for emphasis, not the vocal cords.

A good deal of practicing can be done silently. The score may be studied and the words and notes may be memorized. This is the work to be accomplished when the voice is not in order. This is also the time to listen to others sing, on recordings or at concerts. Listening work is important for your growth. There is no better time to spend at it than when the body is too tired or too ill to sing.

THE IMPORTANCE OF EMOTIONAL AND PHYSICAL HEALTH

Extra rehearsal hours and heavy traveling demands are made upon today's singers. Health is one of the most important assets that a singer must have. It is a good idea to practice hygiene and positive thinking when a student so that as a performer your mind will assume a healthy response to strain and an emotionally sound response to stress. Do not be afraid to ask for help from the medical or the psychiatric profession, but do determine as a student to begin to approach this very challenging field of singing in a vigorous and healthy manner. Emotional health can give one the ability to create a role and then step back into everyday life immediately without strain. This ability to deal with reality in a world where emotional retreats from reality are part of the trade is an extremely difficult skill to develop. It requires a very healthy outlook.

Aside from this built-in difficulty in the field, the ups and downs of a career and the additional stresses that traveling and difficult hours put on one's private life make emotional health very important among the characteristics of a successful performer. The stresses of performance, the demands of technique, memory, and musicianship, plus the usual requirements of everyday living are extreme. Students would do well to prepare their minds and their emotions for this reality.

chapter ix

Rules for Performance

THE FIRST COMMANDMENT:
THOU SHALT NOT BORE

1. Thou shalt not bore by singing:
   a. music that is too hard to sing (at your present level).
   b. a program too difficult in its entirety, and thus a tired second half.
   c. music just barely memorized.
   d. music that is underrehearsed.
2. Thou shalt not bore by singing music:
   a. that is too much alike.
   b. that is too difficult for the audience (that is, an entire program that is too difficult; a few pieces should be a challenge).
   c. that requires too little of the audience.
3. Thou shall not bore by substituting showmanship for vocal technique, or by assuming that good voice is all that is needed in performance.
4. Thou shalt not bore by singing everything with the same vocal color, or with the same look on your face.
5. Thou shalt remember that the hallmark of a true artist is an excitement that is maintained in the least demanding places of the composition.
6. Thou shalt remember how to program.
   a. The audience that sits too long squirms.
   b. Program material should be diversified enough to maintain interest.
   c. Stage organization, stands, chorus changes, and page turners should be thought out and practiced.
   d. Program notes and translations should be short, and to the point so that there is little undue page turning during the concert.
7. Thou shalt:
   a. perform music and text as though you were singing them spontaneously, not reading the words from an unseen card.
   b. present a picture to the audience worth seeing.
   c. acknowledge applause gracefully and happily.
   d. make exits and entrances pleasantly, and pace them evenly.
   e. stand at ease, and yet know that should a mishap occur—an unexpected trip, for instance—the audience will accept it if your embarrassment does not overwhelm them.
   f. be pleased and happy to be singing, and let it show.

GREAT PERFORMANCES ARE INTENSE AND THEY ARE NOT RUSHED

Music is sound. Not dots on a page, not mathematics, not a serious technical exercise, not a composite of players, but the end product: sound. That sound is welded into phrases. It is pulled thin and plumped fat by dynamic changes. Other elements may be involved, but basically music is the manipulation of sound. Unless this sound is artistically handled, it is meaningless. Therefore, the greater the ability of composer and performer to move that sound into meaningful form, the greater the artistic insight involved.

Vocal music is a very particular kind of sound. It is the sound of human personality and it is capable of projecting at a very intimate level joy, sorrow, grief, and the small and large corners of our emotional existence. What is more, the vocal instrument is flexible: in terms of pure sound, it permits a varying picture of the balance of emotions that run through the fiber of humanity.

Listeners want to hear that sound of humanity. They are not particularly eager to hear the triumphs of technique, or voices so controlled that the original sound of life is completely covered. Most listeners do not want to hear pure pedantry, nor are they willing to accept a performance that shows only the virtuosity of acting rather than a good sound. They would like to hear a sound that is the personal contribution of a particular performer.

Art is concerned with the initial insight of an idea and its communication. A sculptor can provide her own communication by presenting her idea through the technique of sculpting. A composer or a dramatist is not so lucky. Each is dependent upon the work of others to present his product. Music unheard communicates to only a few trained souls, but even they are quick to ask for a live performance before giving absolute judgments. A play read is a play read. A play performed is a play.

The burden of performance involves differing and distinctive solutions from each artist. This controversy is a good thing, for it permits several ways of dealing with any problem. However, the performing artist also has responsibilities, such as trying to recognize and to some extent duplicate the composer's intentions. This requires musicianship, knowledge of technique, style, and a literary as well as musical understanding of the work.

THE ABILITY TO PERFORM

We speak of *performing artists*. An artist brings insight into her work. Therefore, we expect a performing artist to delineate that artistry within the confines of her particular performance. These confines are her responsibility to the original manuscript. The singer must learn to handle these symbols of the art as well as the concepts and rules of the arts. It is the manner of the great performing artist to handle the vocal and technical aspect, the musical aspects, and the problems of performance with ease and expertise. She has the responsibility of communicating to an audience.

The primary function of the singer is to produce a good sound. Without that sound the singer is nothing. The primary function of a good performer is to produce a good performance. Without the performance the sound is nothing. The performing personality is as much a gift as is the basic singing sound. This gift may sometimes be discovered within a personality where it has not been noticed before, but it is rarely simulated. It is or it is not. No matter how good a sound the basic talent of a singer can produce, without the scintillation of a good performance, without the life that some people seem to be able to breathe onto a stage, the end product is not salable. This does not mean that a good tone is lost to the world because it is not accompanied by a performing personality. Far from that, for good tones are needed in many places, in the school room, in the choirs, even in professional choirs and choruses and good tones are needed in the minds of appreciators of good music. In general without the ability to perform, to charge a stage with electricity, a professional voice will not sell.

Vocal talent, like all talent, is fairly cheap. Talent willing to withstand the onslaught of years of patient discipline, often with no reward other than an occasional smile or perhaps a very small check for singing "Trees" for the women's society in the local church, is rare. But the rarest of all is the talent that has intelligence, discipline, the gift of a voice, the ability to perform, and the will to succeed.

The ability to perform is closely tied to personality. Some people cannot present themselves broadside to the public with nothing to hide behind, not even the slim veil of an oboe or a flute. This takes courage. For some the courage required is too much; a singer who recognizes this is very wise, and not a professional singer. The voice teacher—in fact, the entire resources of schooling—are at the disposal of those who wish to sing better as well as those who wish to perform. It is the privilege of the student to improve what he has, to go as far as he can in learning to handle his abilities and to use them as he can. Rarely, however, does the honest voice teacher try to push into performance an individual who cannot cope with it, for the results can be tragic.

The cruelest of musical facts in today's world is that the young performer must cope with the "perfect" performances that emanate from television's pretaped performers and from phonograph records. This means that there are very few places in our society for performers to fail, and consequently to relearn, retry, and gradually conquer their profession. Schools try to provide such places, but the danger of the grading system occasionally eliminates even this opportunity.

Ultimately the only place to practice performance is under performance conditions, complete with nerves, jitters, memory slips, stage accidents, and the extra charge of adrenalin that comes from the excitement of the audience. Unfortunately, an American student soon realizes that in our artistic hierarchy there are virtually *no* performance conditions that allow a young classical singer to make mistakes. Most voice studios attempt to provide performance classes for advanced students and similar voice-class experience for beginners. But the next steps are taken outside of the studio, in the university or conservatory atmosphere, where student recitals and solo recitals are given. There is little room for mistakes here, for the students are being graded.

With luck some students can find opportunities—for example, in local churches and social groups—that are not as judgmental as full professional engagements. But as soon as the student is actually ready and lucky enough to find professional engagements at any level, it is necessary for him or her to produce a professional sound and a professional appearance.

APPEARANCE AND ATTITUDE

The importance of a professional appearance and attitude cannot be overstated. Auditioners expect self-confidence and a sureness of manner that will make the audience comfortable. The young student must try to assemble these skills as an immature voice student and couple the learning of stage presence and attitude with vocal instruction. Attitude includes basically accurate musicianship, responsibility about rehearsals, a pleasant demeanor toward colleagues, and a desire to improve even when that means taking criticism.

It is necessary to determine how to walk on and off the stage, and how to make an audience feel that you are in command of the situation. Then they will be able to relax, empathize, and enjoy. In general, performers may overcome *any* stage mishap if they put the audience at ease. A fall is a tragedy only if the performer is overcome by it. Flagstad once tripped during a very hectic performance in Carnegie Hall. At the time she was being picketed ouside the hall. As soon as the audience was assured by her that no bones were broken, the fall was forgotten in her smile and in the common enjoyment of the music.

Slips in memory follow the same rule. Words or music are frequently made up on the spot, with the audience rarely the wiser. It is conceivable that a whole page will suddenly blank out in performance, and it is not inappropriate to walk to the piano and look at the music in order to continue. This is not the end of the world if the singer does not consider it to be so and if he can continue with a look of complete ease with the situation.

Certain aspects of performance can be practiced in the practice rooms. A mirror can tell singers if they have acquired any grimaces or other mannerisms that might upset the audience. They can know their music thoroughly and have it memorized well enough to feel at ease with it. They can have practiced sufficiently with their accompanist so that ensemble, stage manners, and musical awareness are engraved into the performance. It is also necessary to think out such routine matters as calculating the timing of the program, setting the stage for all the performers, getting off and on the stage with many performers, and scheduling the program so that stage changing is kept to a minimum. For example, if one is to use both harpsichord and piano, how can she have this done without a constant change of instruments and still achieve the best type of programming?

At home the performers can become accustomed to the clothing they are to wear on stage. For the women this generally means practicing walking gracefully in long skirts, and understanding how to raise the skirt (preferably with one hand) so as to accomplish graceful battles with stairs and risers of any variety. For both men and women it means assuring themselves that the clothing they have chosen or that is delegated to them is loose enough for proper breath support and for any movement that they are going to have to make during the performance. This may also mean some very close work with the costumer. Period costumes can be very difficult to sing in, and one may have to wear a bone corset through all the rehearsals in order to learn how to find her breath.

In concert the soloist is generally followed by the accompanist when walking on and off the stage. This rule may be changed as seems appropriate in terms of personnel. It is still usually ladies first, although if the soloist is masculine and the accompanist feminine, the rule is not followed as closely as it was a few years ago. Ease and efficiency should have something to do with the final decisions. Bowing or curtsying within the standards of the place and the time is an important thing to practice. American audiences generally expect a bow from both men and women, whereas the curtsy is expected from women in Europe. Common sense and good manners that will make the audience feel at home are the guidelines. Some sort of pleasant recognition of applause is an absolute necessity. Even when every note has been wrong for at least two pages and your voice teacher is squirming because you sang incorrectly and the text was a complete figment of your imagination, the audience that applauds the performance should receive a genuinely appreciative response, including a smile, from the performer.

Stage gestures—operatic, dramatic, or concert—should seem sincere and definite. A pointed hand should have a reason and a good determinable point with all fingers but one closed. General gestures should be made below the face level of the performer unless there is a very dramatic reason for doing otherwise. *All gestures and all stage demeanor should be practiced.* They will not magically appear at performance time.

Most important, the guiding spirit of the performer should be a delight in the music and a strong belief in the intensity of what he is doing. A face should show through its glow the spirit of the music involved. This is far more essential than a gesture here or there. The facial expression along with the stance of the singer should always convey a sense of vitality and sincerity.

Performers perform because they love to perform. They perform music because they have something to say with the music. They give of themselves because they love the music and the performance. When they walk out on the stage their bodies and faces say, "I am glad to be here. I have something exciting to tell you."

DIVERSIFYING THE PROGRAM

A high percentage of the worth of any performance is the result of the spadework and planning that created the program. First, the pieces must be timed. The basic rule is that one's head cannot absorb more than one's seating comfort can endure. The next requirement is diversity. The program should be varied in subject matter, tempo, and vocal color. Here are some typical considerations:

1. Tempo and key changes between songs and between groups of songs.
2. Various styles of music. Such programs are generally designed to start with the oldest music and proceed to contemporary material. This is not always the best order to follow. The endurance of the singer, the timing of the program, and the alternation of tone color and tempi are better considerations.
3. Some programs are given a single theme. This may be topical (war songs), literary (texts by the same poet), or thematical (texts from plays by Shakespeare). Variation must still occur within the selections.
4. Variations in the sound coming from the stage. The possibilities include some obbligato performers or a small chamber group, ensembles, or (if you have the courage) a cappella singing.
5. Variations in the length of groupings and of songs. A rule of thumb the theater generally follows is to present the longer acts early.
6. Variations in the number of intermissions in a program. If the program is particularly intense, they can occur frequently. If it is light and short, it may be expedient to have no intermissions. Intermissions can also occur when it is necessary to change the setup of the stage.

7. There should be some concern with the number of difficult (for the audience) songs to schedule in a program. Few audiences can remain intense during the entire evening. Light music should be included in good programming, and difficult music should appear in a predominantly "light" program.

8. Performers are capable of doing a lot more difficult work in the practice room than they are on the stage. It is very difficult to predetermine just how much more energy it will take to project sound as well as mood to an audience when the singer is nervous. It is much better to underprogram than to overprogram. In recitals, voice teachers sometimes will not enforce this guideline in order to have students discover for themselves that they have attempted too much. There is no teacher as forceful as self-discovery. However, in a professional recital it is extremely important that the last group go as well as the first, that the singer is fresh and ready for it, and that the groups in between do not present such ferocious problems for the singer's technique that additional fears will creep in to disturb the performance.

9. It is a good idea, particularly off college campuses, to include a few numbers that are fairly well known. The audience will enjoy them. Programs ought to present something challenging to an audience, something pleasant, something exciting, and something soothing. The audience should be anxious for more when the program ends. It is disastrous when they are anxious to go home before the last group starts.

PROGRAM NOTES AND TRANSLATIONS

Before the program is printed it must be decided whether to accompany the program with notes or translations. Program translations of the poetry need not be literal. Indeed, such translations are often misleading. On the other hand, comic and dramatic texts do need to have enough conveyed either through translation or notes so that the audience can share in the performance. When translations are printed credit should be given to the translator unless she is the performer. Program notes that can be boiled down to one page are often better than the turning of pages by the audience during the performance. If this is impossible, the notes should be arranged so that page turning takes place between numbers. If notes are used, the house lights must be bright enough to make them usable. With a few texts it may be best to present the audience with both the original language and the English translations. Such texts would include extremely difficult or unknown poetry that is somewhat confused by musical treatment, words that are literally untranslatable into English, and texts that are too complex to understand on one reading. The printing of difficult texts in English is a courtesy. In general, the fewer program notes the better, but these should be enough to inform the average audience of the general drift of the text.

MECHANICAL MATTERS

Certain mechanical matters should be checked before every performance. For even the smallest program the stage lighting should be in order, and the light-board personnel thoroughly informed of the procedures they should follow. It is necessary to check such matters through the stage manager and to be sure that the details of lighting the house and the stage are completely understood. Other considerations are the number of chairs needed, adequate arrangements for a page turner (who has practiced with singer and accompanist), and music stands. If the program is to be recorded, the singer should know where the microphone equipment will be, where wires cross the stage, and whether arrangements have to be made to keep the microphones from obstructing his face. Flower stands should also be placed properly. Are they in danger of turning upside down and ruining a gown or a piano, to say nothing of the performance? Will they fall off the piano while the accompanist is playing "Der Erlkönig"?

Program notes should be prepared in such a way that they may be efficiently passed to the audience. Ushers should know where they are and what to do with them. They should also know the approximate timing of intermissions. Arrangements for receptions, if they are to be public, should be well known to the ushers so that they may help direct traffic.

Above all, is the piano tuned?

It is necessary to check with the accompanist to make sure that the proper music is brought to the recital. This is generally the accompanist's responsibility, but in a chain of recitals given in different locations with several accompanists it becomes the singer's. Since it is always the singer's recital that is being given, the ultimate responsibility for the music is hers. The performer should arrange the bowing procedure with her accompanist before walking out on the stage. Accompanists do at least fifty percent of the work in recital, and they deserve public credit for it. The performer should also make sure that if a page turner is needed, one is available and practiced.

IN CONCLUSION

Many singers are prone to think only of their mistakes during a concert. This is natural when one considers how much time and effort is spent before a recital eliminating musical and vocal mistakes. However, the audience is aware of the good things, the things that went right, the performance that was exciting, and the sound that brought them joy. During a performance the singer should also think of these things. Mistakes become a matter for the practice room. At performance time it is the excitement and the vitality of the music that is the main concern. The performer's energy and talent should be used toward that end. Then both the audience and the performer can enjoy the vocal sound.

chapter x

Theory and the Voice Student

SIGHT SINGING

Most voice students hate sight singing. They are aware not only of what they sing but of how they sing it, whereas the clarinet players sitting next to them in class simply produce pitches. The singer tries to produce tone quality. It is more difficult for the poor soprano to sing the fourth C–F than it is for the clarinet player, because she knows that she is also accounting for a shift in tone quality. Singers are fundamentally aware of these difficulties, but rarely can they verbalize them enough to confront the sight-singing exercise and either lick the problem at hand or use only a pitched sound for the class. Most singers refuse to do the latter; after all it is their vocal tone quality that makes them singers, and that is what they wish to have heard.

Sight singing on the job, then, becomes a major problem, since the singer is already so inhibited about sight singing in the classroom. But it is a necessity. Singers should not assume that because of the beauty of their vocal instrument they need not sight-sing. The places where one earns money for singing—commercials, church music, new music—demand a good level of sight singing. There is very little place in today's market for the singer who cannot accomplish a degree of sight singing.

Sight singing is the opposite of ear training. One can go to the theory lab and listen to ear-training tapes for practice, but what can one do about practicing sight singing? Obviously, once a passage becomes practiced it can no longer be sight-sung. An answer must be found for a singer must learn. One way is choral singing in which the singer can practice and be corrected without undue tension.

A concert choir in which sight singing is a matter of tension is not the best place to learn. Tension is the enemy of good singing, and many a singer has had vocal fatigue after a session in which the director has been either extremely demanding or sarcastic. The local church choir is often a better place to learn and practice sight singing.

Sight singing can also be practiced in the practice room with new music. Whatever the environment, the most important skill to learn in sight singing is to recognize what you have sung. If you can sight-sing a line from a song, you must realize what you have sung in terms of intervals or harmonic structure.

Just about any method of sight singing will work as long as it is consistent, and consistently practiced. After one has become fluent in one method it is fairly easy to skip to another method. The original method must be solidly practiced and known, however. Remember that the most important part of sight singing is the rhythm: one can miss the pitch and regroup, but when rhythm is missed the whole piece is wrong.

UNDERSTANDING BASIC THEORY

It is also necessary to understand the basic theory underlying a piece of music that is being studied. It is sometimes difficult for voice students to appreciate the feeling for harmony, for they bury themselves with the vocal line and the intervals. Consequently, when the piece is put together with the accompaniment it is very difficult for them to appreciate the feel of the total structure.

One cannot completely condemn this approach. Indeed, in contemporary music atonality and unrelated intervals (unrelated in terms of a tonality) make it almost a necessity. However, one must consider not only the vocal line but also the rhythmic structure, the harmonic implications, the harmonic rhythm, and the form of a piece.

Let's examine the eighteenth-century song at the end of the chapter. Only the bass and vocal lines have been reprinted. The latter is fairly simple. Notice that it starts on the fifth degree of the scale, a note one easily arrives at by singing a beginning arpeggio in e minor. Measure 13 outlines a diminished seventh, not always the easiest jump in the world, but since the C is a member of a minor chord (a minor, indicated by the first pitches in the bass and soprano lines) and the D sharp belongs to the B-major chord under it, that seventh is easy to sing because the harmony lets us expect it. The ear hears it well, and this might be a time to retrain your ear to what a falling diminished seventh sounds like and feels like on these pitches. Measure 14 continues to outline the B chord. The E is found easily from the D-sharp, and the melody line of this measure fits well into the harmony of the dominant chord. Since the passage is written in e minor, the sense of tonality should carry one through. There is a cadence in measure 29 in E major. A number of arpeggios sung during warm-ups or for other technical reasons can be done in the minor as well as the major mode in order to help the ear become sure of the difference.

In the next part of the piece there is a recurrence of the dotted rhythms, which by this time the eye and the brain should be able to deal with easily. The pitches are not difficult if one senses that from measure 32 onwards the harmonic structure is reflecting in general the circle of fifths. Measure 32 starts with a G-sharp diminished chord resolving to a minor. The E major in measure 33 falls to an A^7 and then to a D^7 going to a G. (Measures 35–43 constitute a sequence.) From G the composer skips back to the parallel major of the relative minor of G. E major then drops to A then to the sixth of A, F-sharp, which falls down a fifth to B and then to e minor (measure 44), which falls to A^7 and a cadence in D. The next section (measure 48) starts on the D^7 so there is no problem in finding the beginning note of that phrase. The sequence then continues through the key of G and

through e minor until the final cadence in e minor. All of the notes above are easily within a step-wise progression of sequences and skips within a chord, with an occasional appoggiatura from above to a chord member.

Remember that the melodic line as well as the harmonic line is generally created by the composer so as to reflect the poet's intentions. The composer expects the performer to pay enough attention to the harmonic shifts and compositional structure so that the piece may be made more meaningful by the performer's interpretation. For instance, the ascending sequence from measure 35 through measure 43 does not rise enough in pitch to allow the higher voice to become a good deal more brilliant naturally. That is, acoustics tell us that higher notes are more easily heard than low ones at the same dynamic level, but with this slight rise in pitch it is necessary for the performer to intensify the sequence as it goes upward for the proper effect.

The rhythmic motive, a dotted eighth followed by a sixteenth and then by a quarter note, is repeated so often that even at a largo pace it could become very jumpy unless the singer realized that the composer is repeating the text (see measure 48 to the end) and that such jumpiness is out of character. Therefore, it must be sung accurately and smoothly. Vocally, this will mean "not pushed" and on the lighter side of the voice, just as an ornament would be sung. The sound should float in the low registers of the voice without becoming too full.

Another point: the composer sets out in the first two measures of the piece to give a strong line to the accompaniment. That phrase, then, is very important to the composer. It appears again under the beginning of the vocal line. The singer has a held note over it. The rising quarter-note phrase in the bass is more important than the held note of measure 12 in the singer's line. It would behoove the singer to start this long note softly so that the audience will hear the accompaniment. The singer can then take this note and swell into it while moving into measure 13 thereby establishing a good, vital sound before skipping down to that diminished seventh. The rising phrase in the accompaniment occurs once again under the repetition of the first theme in the key of G. Again the singer has a held note, and again the soft beginning with a slight swell is indicated by the music. The held note of measure 22 is not over the rising phrase, however, and it is conceivable that a singer would wish to start this tone louder and let the note become softer in order to provide some contrast. The cadence in E major at the beginning of measure 29 signifies that there is a change of character in the next section of the piece. A new tone color or a sudden surge of energy might be used to produce the vocal change that the composer has indicated in his harmonic structure.

Thus, an understanding of how the composer put the piece together will help the singer interpret the piece. Knowledge of music theory and structure helps sight singing: it is always easier to sing a major triad, regardless of its tonal setting, if only one recognizes it as a major triad. It is also easier to sing certain leaps when they are outlined by the chord movement of the piece *if* one recognizes what the chord movement is.

Every piece, new or old, can teach sight singing, ear training, harmony, and musical understanding if one's brain is at work as well as one's mouth.

O Give Me the Comfort

Maurice Greene (1695-1755)

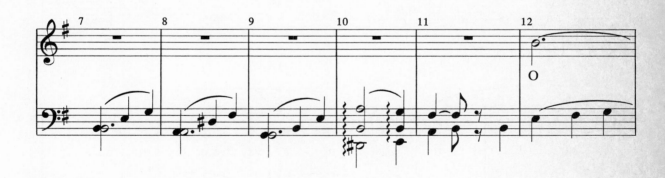

L. Stanley Roper, ed., *Oxford Choral Songs From the Old Masters: Unison*, no. 335 (London: Oxford University Press, 1923). Reprinted by permission of the publisher.

chapter xi

Listening for the Vocal Sound

Sound is the singer's chief medium. It is his ability to manipulate sound to its most efficient resonance and greatest dramatic effect that allows the singer to intensify a performance to a salable and competitive commodity. In order to achieve this goal, the singer must know what he wishes to hear and how to translate this sound through his vocal apparatus into the ears of those listening to him. Before he can make the descision of the type of sound he is after, he must have a repertoire of sounds in his ear from which to choose. He must, in short, learn to listen to himself and his own sound. In order to do this, a task complicated by the fact that the singer hears his own voice differently than he hears the voices of others, it is necessary to learn how to listen to sound in general.

LISTENING TO SOUND

For many people, listening to music is simply a sensual delight. They allow music to wrap itself about them and to fill their ears and mind with sound, but they have little or no active intellectual involvement. This may be a perfectly legitimate way for music lovers to enjoy music, but not the music students. Students must know the whys and wherefores of their listening pleasure, for one cannot produce what one does not understand in some fashion. Since we are dealing with the sound of the voice, it is essential that we understand that sound and recognize variations in vocal sound if we are to produce them. It is also appropriate that we as musicians understand the musical logic and form behind sound. Such understanding will enhance our scholarly pleasure. Understanding the vocal sound will enhance our performance.

A great deal of music listening in our society takes place on a nonhearable level. Muzak, the car radio, television background music, music to dine by—all this is accepted but not heard. It does not satisfy any purpose other than to cover up other noise. Most people do not hear it; they merely miss it when it is absent.

This habit of not hearing is so prevalent that the musician who has overcome it becomes almost psychotic when trying to keep up a conversation at dinner with Muzak gliding around and about her. Her ears demand that she listen, but good manners demand that she participate in conversation with those who are not even aware of the sound. Unfortunately, too many of us have developed to an extreme the non-listening habit. This bad habit must be torn down and replaced with proper ear training that will challenge singers to improve and to widen their repertoire of sounds.

An ear may never be able to hear much of anything in vocal sound because of its particular physical structure. Such ears do not stay in music very long. Most ears can be trained to hear something. In fact the awareness that one ought to be listening for something is occasionally enough to start the process.

The nearest record library has many sounds. Most of them can be classified at any point in a student's development as good, better, or best sounds. Some of the sounds (unfortunately) may be classifed as bad or even lousy sounds. The first step in listening is to ascertain the difference between the bad sound and the good-better-best variety. No one can do this for anyone else. The listener must train his own ear. Sometimes discriminating questions or discussion can help an ear to listen harder, but in the long run the judgment of the listener at any given moment is the most important consideration.

After some discernment has been noted between sounds liked and those unliked, there comes the level of trying to verbalize why one sound is of one group and not the other. It is better at this point *not* to be swayed too much by the judgment of others. It may be that differences in vocabulary in the description of sounds make one verbalization appear very much out of the ordinary acceptance level. A slow and careful buildup of vocabulary may straighten out a good many differences.

WHAT TO LISTEN FOR IN VOCAL SOUNDS

Evenness of Tone

We listen, and what we hear becomes a conscious and unconscious repertoire of sounds that will affect the sounds we make. But as beginners what should we listen for? We listen for the things that a singer tries to produce: relaxed quality, something that feels easy to listen to, an even tone that sounds as though it belongs to the same person throughout the range. In a very good voice we take that evenness for granted, but in the learning voice we are able to hear individuals who sing duets with themselves, sometimes even a trio. It will help at times to listen to recordings by different artists of the same composition so that we can understand how each of the different singers approaches the same vocal problems. It also helps to listen with the score in hand so that the ear has a visual guide to what is being done and why.

Quality of Tone

Then there is the quality of the tone itself—the basic sound of any voice, predetermined by certain acoustic factors of the resonating system. There is also an acceptance/rejection factor that the human ear administers unconsciously to the voice it is helping to produce. Quality of tone, therefore, varies from singer to singer because of natural reasons. It varies from era to era because of the acceptance factor of any age. It varies from the "pop" field to the "art" field because of the acceptance standards of the listeners. There is, however,

very little essential difference in any of these variables when basic vocal production is being considered. Basically, both pop and art singers must breathe correctly and use their voices efficiently if they are to remain in their field. Thus, a very basic conception of good tone quality can be found by the ear that is willing to listen for similarities between pop artists (those who have been in the field long enough to assure that their voices will not fade away) and singers of opera or art song. In the beginning, it is true, an ear may be overwhelmed by the differences between the two sounds, but gradually that same ear becomes able to hear the similarities to understand them.

Vibrato and Wobble

We look for warmth and coolness in voices. We also become quickly aware of vibrato (an even variation of pitch that gives it warmth) and wobbles (an uneven fluctuation of the voice that is apt to distort pitch and vocal line). A straight tone—one without a vibrato—can become a tense or boring sound when overused. A singer's vibrato can be trained to a specific rate by very mechanical means, and this training is dependent upon ear training. In his experiments in the 1930s Carl Seashore trained vibratos to a given rate. Normally we seem to wish to hear five to seven vibrations per second, for this rate appears to be comfortable for the listener.

Slowly the listening ear may be able to discern that the wobble in some voices is caused by poor technique, or by a choice on the part of a particular singer who likes it and uses it, particularly in pop music, for a type of ornamentation. Sometimes wobbles get completely out of hand and are incurable. In time the listening ear can hear most of these things. They become as natural as the discernment of the sharping or flatting of pitches.

Breath Control, Agility and Dynamics

A singer's breath control is fairly obvious in recordings. Sometimes a score and a knowledge of the demands of a piece are necessary for the listener to fully appreciate what the singer has accomplished. Agility and the use of dynamics are two other factors that are fairly easy to hear. Sometimes poor earphones or poor equipment in general distort the dynamic levels in a recording, but with today's level of reproduction one can generally hear dynamic change to a very sensitive degree. Agility—the ability to accomplish runs and ornaments—can be manifested in several ways. Acute listeners become aware of these different styles of articulation. The appreciation of the sound difference often arouses the singer to give these variances a try in the practice room. This type of copying and exploring is admirable.

Excitement

A voice should be exciting. A performance should be intense, with an authority that holds the attention and excitement of the listener. This is a difficult concept to put into the words that compare one performance with another. A voice should be warm without a rasp or an edgy sound.

Diction

Then there is the text and the diction. Every singer has peculiarities with diction, some of which will be helpful to the listening student. Diction often is a basic clue to the excitement of a performance or of a particular tone color. More than that, diction, particularly English diction, is something the ear has listened to before. Therefore the ear has a point of reference, and as long as more demands are made upon the ear to become disciplined and exact in the skill of listening to diction, it is already on a known road. This road should include some copying of sounds in the practice room. It may be found, for instance, that diction leads a student to perform with a different tone color, or a different feeling for placement. This in turn gives her insight into the listening process, and the next time she listens she will do so with a more acute ear to the slight changes in diction that the performer uses both for effect and for technique.

Questions to Ask

There are questions that the listener can ask: How dramatic is the singer? Is the diction understandable? Does the singer take a phrase and mold sound and diction into communication? Does the phrase say something? How about the tone quality? What about the style? Does the voice quality fit the style in which the piece was written? Does a

pop singer miss the rhythm or use a voice that is too sophisticated for the style of the piece? Is a Baroque piece being misused by a voice tuned into the darker sounds of the scale that might be more appropriate to Wagner? A voice should be able to convey the colors of tone the composer had in mind. Comparing recordings of the same material sung by different performers gives added insight into the vocal solutions to these problems.

LISTENING TO OURSELVES AS OTHERS DO

Vocalists have a problem that few other performing artists have: they have to build not only their technique but also their instrument. To a large extent, vocalists cannot define their technique until their instrument is mature. This means years of vocal study that incorporates instrument building as well as vocal technique. Ear training is also a matter of study and maturation.

This pertinent fact is difficult for the beginning student to grasp. For above and beyond the maturity factor, every vocalist listens to his own performance differently than he would to an instrument that is being played. The vocalist listens through bone conduction to a sound that will be judged by listeners listening through air conduction. The singer is never completely able to disassociate himself from the instrument: his own body. This makes the listening lesson more difficult, but more vital. How can one hear someone else's voice through the air and then transcribe that sound into his own body, which is monitored by a different type of hearing? The answer is "With difficulty." However, it can be done, and the ability to discern differences in the performances of others leads to a peculiar kind of empathy with other singers that makes the listening student wish to use his body and his voice in different ways. This type of hearing takes time to develop. With patience the training of the ear and listening ability will develop into an understanding of the production of voice.

The process of tonal ear training is as difficult as the process of classroom ear training and sight singing. In many cases that kind of ear training is so intent upon teaching musical form and the technical aspects of composition that the physical sound of the music is overlooked. This is particularly true in universities, where there is such concern with the technical side of performance. Fingers, keyboards, and vocal placement can all become ends within themselves instead of means to create listenable and desirable sound. The ability to distinguish fifths from fourths can become more important than the ability to hear the difference between an exciting sound and a dull one.

The desirable product of a musical performance is music that communicates. It is not a bad idea to begin by listening to what one has been hearing for a long time, the voices of contemporaries speaking and singing, and the sound of any music that is known, in order to increase the ear's ability to discriminate differences in vocal sound. Perhaps the voice patterns (speech patterns) of two friends could be compared. From there the growth of the ear can begin. Interacting with more sounds at the same time one is learning to produce sounds can lead to some challenges that in turn will lead to more learning. It also helps to hear other voices in the same phase of learning that the student is in. Then the questions concerning the differences among several voices, all of which are at the same level of production that the listener's voice has attained, become more significant. Questions then can include What do you hear? What is the difference between voice A and voice B? Why does one voice appeal more than another? Is there some reason based in the voices that makes the difference? From questions such as these the ear can learn, and in turn teach the listener to be a better singer.

The development of a student's ability to copy sounds she has heard and finally to achieve a repertoire of her own sounds appropriate for performance is a goal for listening. This demands that ear training permit one to hear oneself as others hear oneself. It will be found that most of this ability is linked to a "feeling" about the production of a given tone, that every room has a different acoustical ambiance that affects that tone. Consequently, when listening to oneself sing, one must be aware of the feeling of the tone as well as the sound. Trying out the way a listened-to tone "feels" within the body of the listener sometimes helps to answer the problem of how the voice sounds in any ambience.

A LISTENING GUIDE

Listening, as much as possible to as many different sounds as possible, presents the singer with a key to the many vocal responses that can be made musically (and nonmusically). These sounds should be in the repertoire of the singer's ear if they are to be available for her to seek out as singing tones for herself. The listening lesson is basic in the development of skills and vocal sounds. It is also basic in the growth of musical understanding and in the broadening of the listener's outlook and outreach.

The following guide is one outline that may be of value in learning how to listen.

Name of recording _____

   I like it _____

   I don't like it _____

Name of artist _____

  Adjectives for the Voice [those given are merely samples]

  Tone [dark, warm, bright, forward, back]

  Color [dull, changeable, interesting] _____

  Diction [understandable, choppy, mushy] _____

  Interpretation [dramatic, lyric, comic] _____

Style [fitting, illogical] _____

Technique [even scale, vibrato, agile, wobbly, raspy, hooty, breathy] _____

The Performance

The goal of the performance _____

Characterization _____

Mood _____

Did the performance succeed? _____

I liked (did not like) this performance and/or this voice because:

_____

_____

_____

_____

_____

chapter xii

Phrasing

Phrasing is the ability to turn notes into melody and melody into song. It is analogous to turning words into sentences and sentences into paragraphs. Vocal phrasing adds the complication of words to musical phrasing. A great deal of the literature also adds the element of dramatization.

The process of tension and release that is the energy and drive behind music comes from the use of harmony, pitch, rhythm, and dramatic interpretation of the composer's intentions. The requirements of reproducing the text are similar: word groupings, word meanings,, and the essence of the complete text. The dramatic requirements include the understanding of character and/or situation plus the ability to color the voice to produce effective dramatic sound.

The best phrasing depends upon a thorough knowledge of all of these separate entities and an ability to provide both vocal technique and artistic insight. In short: build notes into music. A phrase requires the thought that sees the entire concept through to the end, rather than a production of individual notes. It needs a steady supply of breath, and control that will regulate that breath into a meaningful melody. The singer must interpret vocal phrases musically without impairing the text or destroying the dramatics of the piece. Composers indicate through harmony, pitch, and rhythm where phrases should be heightened and where they should be relaxed.

Although music is sound and not a technique, there are certain patterns of thinking that will help to create the sound that is needed. The body is the vocal instrument. The energy behind that instrument is breath. Breath begins before a phrase is started and carries through each note until after the final note is completed. In phrasing music the singer must carry the sound on her breath. The diction is carried on the line of musical sound. Since this sound is present in the formation of vowels, and since the consonants are sources of noise, it is necessary to eliminate much of the noise in order not to destroy the flow of sound necessary for the musical line. On the other hand, diction is needed for the text. Therefore it is the quality of the noise, not the quantity, that is the concern of the vocalist. In other words, short but crisply and sharply spoken consonants will permit the vocal line to be carried at maximum efficiency under the necessities of speech. To this end exercises in diction are given on page 39. They must be practiced with the intention of creating skills that will enable the singer to define groups of words within the phrase without destroying the musical line or the meaning of the text.

THE ONSET OF A TONE

The onset of the tone that begins a phrase begins with support. Support and the proper easy breath are necessary before the sound can begin. This support is maintained throughout the phrase and is released only when the singer takes a breath and initates the tones for the next phrase. Most tones should begin with a sigh. All high tones should begin softly. They may, of course, become loud very quickly, but they begin with a sound similar to a sigh, and they begin high in the feeling of placement.

Exercises for the onset of a tone may be done in the following manner. With the center of the tip of the tongue positioned against the top teeth, produce a long, steady [ssss] with a long, gently used, unobvious breath. Then start a note with the consonant [s] (the notes in this part of the exercise should be placed in an easy portion of the range). Commence the tone softly, and then crescendo, decrescendo, and crescendo again without tension in the throat and with the feeling and flow of a sigh. Note the feeling of an easy breath going across the lips. The length of the exercise depends on your ability and maturity. Each time you repeat the exercise assure yourself that there is enough support—an outward and upward motion of the bottom of the rib cage, spritely posture, and low abdominal stature to maintain that support—to insure an easy tone. Find this support as you are taking the breath, before producing the sound.

Dundee

Text: William Cowper

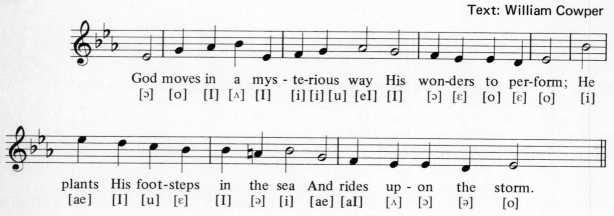

Then choose a phrase from the literature. As an example let's consider a tune from the *Scottish Psalter* (1615). Starting with the syllable [s] followed by either the vowel [ɛ] or the vowel [ae], initiate the first tone and carry it through the phrase. Each succeeding tone should begin where its immediate predecessor was terminated, as far as dynamic level and intensity is concerned. Sing the entire phrase as though it were actually one tone. That is, continue the sigh through the phrase, letting the intensity of sound go from one note to the next without perceptible differences in tone and magnitude. First attempt the phrase without any use of diction. Then use the vowel sounds of the words, but not the consonants. When you have accomplished this without a break in tone or a cessation of voice or intensity throughout the phrase, add diction.

The onset of any tone should become a very conscious focus of singer's technique. If it is too aggressive and heavy, the tone cannot lead to anything but a vocal disaster and musical distortion. The onset of a tone must allow the singer to manipulate tone into a phrase; it must grant him the room to move and the agility with which he can accomplish this. Consequently, the continual attention to onset, particularly the onset of a tone beginning a phrase, should become a learned reflex in a singer's technique. The onset of each phrase must not use all or too much of the breath. If it does, the remainder of the phrase will be awkward at best.

BREATHING

A phrase uses one sweep of breath in a continuous flow of energy. The diction occasionally requires a stop for another supply of breath. The smaller the stop the better, but the sweep of energy continues through the stop. Outside influences—that is, influences that are not musical—will affect phrasing. These include the demands of the text, the ability to overcome technical problems in the production of voice, and the dramatic requirements of the composition and the stage. In general there should be no cessation of energy throughout the phrase. Short notes should not be shortchanged. The dynamic level of the phrase continues from one note to the next, the latter note picking up at the same level the former one used. A note held may be swelled into the next note, but the next note again starts where the former one finished.

Phrases swell from one tone to the next, much as though they were a held note.

Rests within the phrase should be incorporated into the energy line of the phrase without a large gap for gasping for a breath. The notes on either side of the rest should not be treated dissimilarly, unless, of course, the composer requests this.

Repeated notes, with or without repeated syllables, are difficult to handle. They require much the same treatment as rests. Sometimes the vocal requirements of the text are helpful in separating the notes. Sometimes they are not, and it is up to the performer to decide whether he should opt for a very flowing line that uses as little pause in the flow of breath between the notes as possible, or whether he should use stops between these notes. The latter technique is slightly similar to the catch breath.

Breathing is extremely important for the creation of vocal line. If the rib cage is trained to stay in a floating position without tension in the shoulder area, subtle breathing can occur that will permit the singer to create long lines without interruption for long and noisy gasps of air. The proper posture also creates the conditions necessary for a catch breath. The catch breath is actually no breath at all, but rather a cessation of air going outwards that permits the lungs to recover a bit and continue the phrase. The most likely places for catch breaths are:

1. in the formation of an initial consonant, where the singer may pause for just a second before actually sounding it.
2. at the time of jumps upward of more than a fourth. This is the same manner in which a Baroque keyboard artist articulates such jumps.
3. before the initial note within a sequence.
4. after a tied note.
5. at cadences.

Catch breaths are best practiced under the actual demands of the music. To some degree they must be fitted into the technique and personal interpretations of the singer. Consider the following four examples (* indicates possible breath). The first illustrates leaps upward, the second, leaps downward at a tie; the third, a sequence; and the fourth, an initial consonant and cadence.

Die Armen Will der Herr Umarmen (Cantata 186)

J. S. Bach

er schen - ket ih - nen aus er -

Bach Gesellschaft edition, Vol. 37, p. 144, mm. 11-12.

Die Armen Will der Herr Umarmen (Cantata 186)

J. S. Bach

Aus — Er - bar - - men

(*) alternatives
Bach Gesellschaft edition, p. 144. mm. 2-4.

Es halt' es mit der blinden Welt (Cantata 94)

J. S. Bach

Kann ich reich und se - - - lig

Bach Gesellschaft edition, Vol. 22, p. 123, mm. 9-11.

Gerechter Gott, ach, rechnest Du (Cantata 89)

J. S. Bach

So wer-de ich zum Heil
Bach Gesellschaft edition, Vol. 20, p. 192, mm. 14-16.

TAPERING THE ENDING NOTES

The most important skill in phrasing is the tapering of the ending notes into a graceful melodic line. The one word that seems to present a great danger to singers in this respect, be they solo or chorus members, is *alleluia*. It is apt to sound like a succession of barking dogs: AlleluIA, alleluIA. When sung in this fashion, the last syllable is bumped and is usually followed by a gasp for breath that adds to the overemphasis of a weak syllable at the end of the line.

One frequently hears phrases that are regularly bumped at the end. They completely destroy the composer's intentions and the poet's as well. In English and German, languages that lack feminine endings, this tendency becomes very noticeable and annoying. Certain rhyme schemes complicate this problem. For instance, the diphthongs in the rhymes *day-may* and *night-light* require skillful handling. They are usually important words and must have energy. Yet they are found at the end of the line, when a singer is running out of breath, and in a place where the phrase should have a graceful ending. The ending consonants of German *nacht-sacht* require skillful manipulation so that they fall lightly after the cessation of sound.

Wie rafft ich mich auf

Johannes Brahms

mit ih-nen der Mond in be - ru - hig - ter Pracht,   sie

fun - kel - ten sacht_ in der Nacht, in der Nacht
Brahms Album, (Frankfort: C. F. Peters), vol. III, p. 60.

This entire poem makes much of the *-acht* sound in rhyming position. If this sound is "bumped" in any manner, the softness of the night, that is *nacht*, will become too disturbed to portray the meaning of the poem.

AVOIDING DISTORTION

Phrasing is often distorted unnecessarily by the creation of dotted notes. Singers will overdot notes, leaving no energy or sound for the shorter values. The combining of repeated notes on the same pitch is a trouble spot where one must maintain sufficient lightness of tone quality in order to be able to articulate each note individually without losing the effect of unity. The sound rides through the vowel formation to the next consonant within a continuous phrase. The following exercise should be thought of as a continuous sound on one note; the singer thinks merely of a change of pitch. There should be no "ha-ha" articulations or breaks in the sound. The energy should continue through the dotted note, regardless of the speed taken to perform the phrase.

When a word is substituted for a single vowel sound—*check*, for instance— the *ch* is sounded before the initial musical sound and the *ck* is put on after the musical sound of the final note is dropped. If the word has two syllables, the first is carried on the vowel until the vowel changes, the consonant grouping is quick and decided, and the remainder of the phrase is carried on the second vowel:

ha - - - - - tche - - - - - - - - ck

The sound should build an arch from one note to the next, *not*:

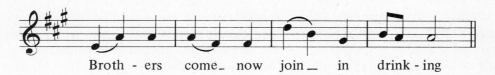

This is particularly important in singing phrases in which the note values are uneven and there is a tendency to equate short notes with soft sound.

Should the rhythm and the word accent coincide on a strong beat measure after measure in obvious fashion, a singsong phrasing can be the unfortunate result if the performer does not give particular attention to evening out the obvious:

Broth - ers   come _ now   join _   in   drink - ing

This can easily be heard as "bro- come join drink" with other notes merely thrown in, often in the wrong rhythm, sometimes completely inaudible, but in a pattern that suggests that what is really being sung is ONE two three, ONE two three. It will sound as though the singer is keeping time with his voice and paying no attention to musical considerations. The line should flow throughout the sentence, and the musical sound should flow with intensity from one note to the next, emphasizing the strong words within the context of the musical rhythms and dynamics demanded by the song. Even though this is a robust song, and hardly one for delicate nuances, if one is to issue a cheerful invitation, the tone of the phrase should suggest the invitation.

It is also helpful to carry through phrases containing word changes within musical phrasing that leaps in arpeggios. It is very easy to overaccent the first of each of these groups, and when this is done the median notes will lose sound, and drop their rhythmic values. If the phrase is to be meaningful, it must be consistent with the rhythmical values, regardless of pitch or diction or placement. At times this means actually diminishing the dynamic level of stressed notes to insure that the entire phrase will sound equal. This must be remembered in handling melodies in which there is a great gap between the highest note and the lowest. High notes naturally sound louder than lower ones. Consequently, in phrasing such a melody the singer must consciously pay attention to the lower notes so that they will sound at the same dynamic level as the higher ones.

Here is an étude that combines a number of the problems discussed above.

To   a song   of   joy___   add   a   song   of   sor - row,

one for to-day, ___ one for to-mor-row, To the thrill of

love ___ add a cry ___ of fear, One far ___ a-

way, far ___ a-way. One ___ quite ___ near.

INTEGRATING WORDS AND MUSIC

Phrasing means that music ought to say something. It should not be just a pileup of notes. Words and sentences should also be turned into something literate. Notes should be turned into a telling vocal and musical line. As the phrases gather they become melodic images whose tension and release are meaningful to the listener. The singer, however, must worry about the words and the musical phrase. So there will be times when the singer has to decide whether to bend the musical phrase to accommodate the sentence structure, or vice versa. The best music from the vocalist's point of view combines the work of composer and poet so that the phrases coincide. Some musicians, such as Hugo Wolf, took immense pains to insure that this would happen. Other musicians were not worried about the effect of the music on the word structure.

In some compositions this emphasis on one of the ingredients of song over another depends upon the style of music characteristic of the era. For instance, although Baroque music emphasized word painting within the musical structure, that structure in the late Baroque and the Classical era was fundamentally a structure growing from musical rather than poetic form. Cadences and the rise and fall of the musical line are more important than the text. Occasionally the music bends to the dramatic, and listeners are aware that their ears listen for the finalities and intricacies of the form because of the story's demand. In a Handel aria the text will be repeated until the musical form is finished. Bach's runs are written in sequences that are musically rather than textually oriented. This does not detract from the total work of art, but it is necessary for the performer to know that this style demands that the music be given first consideration. The works of the realistic-opera school do not always place the music first; text or stage developments are often of prime importance in Wagner and Puccini. Early English lute songs lean heavily on the structure and the sound of the text. Often the musician was a poet, if not *the* author of the particular piece he was performing. Here the rhythmic values of the poetry are overwhelming.

The first two verses of Robert Herrick's "Bid Me to Live" read:

> Bid me to[1] live, and I will live
> > Thy protestant[2] to be
> Or bid me love, and I will give
> > A loving heart to thee.
> A heart as soft, a heart as kind,
> > A heart as sound[3] and free
> As in the whole world thou canst[4] find
> > That heart I'll give to thee.

Various versions of the Herrick text on this page show the following changes:
  1. but
  2. votary
  3. soundly
  4. canst not find
There are five verses in the original, which is entitled "Love's Votary."

The musician Henry Lawes has set each verse in two phrases so that the text now reads:

Bid me to live, and I will live thy protestant to be
Or bid me love, and I will give a loving heart to
   thee.

This means that the pause, or the lift, before the ending of each line in the poem is not necessarily to be found in the song. It also means that the singer is confronted with some long phrases, and must determine to catch a few breaths at commas where obviously the poet did not want them:

Bid me to live (breathe) and I will live. . .
Or bid me love (breathe). . . .

This option is almost mandatory within the structure of the second verse, where another set of commas provides additional breathing space:

A heart as soft (breathe) a heart as kind (breathe)
A heart as sound and free (breathe)
As in the whole world thou canst find (breathe)
That heart I'll give to thee.

It would be better to combine the wishes of poet and musician and not breathe for the entire verse. That may be an impossible option for the music is fairly stark and relentless, with little recovery time:

Bid Me to Live

Henry Lawes
Text: Robert Herrick

Bid me to live, and I will live Thy pro-tes-tant to be
A heart as soft, a heart as kind, A heart as sound and free
Bid that heart stay, and it will stay To hon-or thy de cree;

Or bid me love, and I will give A lov-ing heart to thee.
As in the whole world thou canst find That heart I'll give to thee.
Or bid it lan-guish quite a-way And't shall do so for thee.

The Treasury of Music (London: John Playford, 1669), Republished: (Ridgewood, N.J.: Gregg Press, 1964), p. 30.

Goethe was known to like strophic songs and he felt that it was the performer's prerogative to alter the verses in order to take care of any demands from the text or the drama. In "Bid Me to Love" it becomes necessary, for instance, to unite the phrase ". . . it will stay To honor thy decree." This is not as important in the first two verses. There the skillful performer will alter phrases to produce an intelligible text and an interesting musical line. He will provide the efficient and clear *l* sound to underline the poet's intentions in paralleling *bid-live* and *bid-love*. However, it is easy to lose all thought of producing a flowing melodic line in a piece as wordy as this. Every note has its syllable; there are no melismas. The entire composition could sound like a poem declaimed to music rather than a song. A skillful performer will be needed here to produce musical line as well as poetic line.

This rather simple song presents two phrases of six measures each, antecedent and consequent phrases. The first builds to a musical climax, and the second returns from that climax. The poetic high point can be found at the musical cadences in verse one, but not necessarily in the other verses. It becomes apparent that one of the phrasing devices that can underlie the musical and poetic effect will be a tapered, deliberately softened sound, rather than greater dynamics at the ending of the second phrase. Intensity and energy level will remain constant. Thus, from the form of the piece the phrasing and dynamics are more or less dictated. Notice also that at the first cadence there is a dotted eighth note followed by a short sixteenth. In order to maintain the sweep of the phrasing one could sing this sixteenth note quite smoothly, or a small catch before the "to" might enable the singer to finish the phrase in one breath and set off the words "to be," in keeping with the entire poetic effect of the song. It must be done gracefully and lightly so that the context of the music is not destroyed.

The second phrase builds to a melodic climax in its third and fourth measures. In the first two verses this phrasing does not coincide with the poetry. There the singer must bend the musical intention to fit the poetic one and soften the climax of the line so that it fits into a gentle arch of dynamics rather than a forceful one.

This short song—indeed, every song—provides much to contemplate. Phrasing is an essential element in the performance of any song.

ORNAMENTATION

The subject of Baroque ornamentation is a broad one more suited to history books than a beginning book on singing. The articles by Westrup in Grove's Dictionary and Aldrich in the Harvard Dictionary are very informative. The *idea* of ornamentation is an inherent attitude toward singing held by the singer who is a free, technically secure stylist. And what does that mean? An Ella Fitzgerald recording will let you hear more than the printed page. This is improvisation within the jazz style of our own era. With a feeling for jazz improvisation in mind, and a knowledge of some of the rules of the age of the music you are singing—particularly the standard "don'ts"—coupled with enough listening to good artists singing music from that age, a student may begin to feel the spots that need to be ornamented.

For instance, one of the secure rules of Baroque literature is the cadence trill: when at a strong cadence the vocal line rests on the third or fifth tone of the dominant chord (of that cadence), particularly when it is a dotted note, it must be trilled. After extended acquaintance with this concept, the necessity for the trill becomes apparent. However, beginning students are advised to learn music without ornamentation until the rhythm and structure of the piece are secure, and then, within the bounds of their ability, to add the ornamentation that is applicable. It is always better to err on the side of too little rather than too much ornamentation.

All ornaments should be used in keeping with the overall rhythmic characteristics and atmosphere of the piece. The signs that indicate vocal ornamentation change in meaning from era to era. Consequently, it is a good idea to check either of the dictionaries mentioned above for the meaning that was current at the time the sign was originally used. However, some of the more frequent vocal ornaments are indicated below.

The *acciaccatura* (now called a *grace note*). The singer forms this ornament by stealing time from the previous beat. The main note comes on the beat. The start of the tone is light and high. Any accent comes on the main note.

The *appoggiatura*. Here, time is stolen from the main note. The ornament is the accented note.

The *turn*. Changes from the expected tonality will be shown above or below the sign indicating the note to be changed. The turn should be sung within the given time segment in a rhythm and manner in keeping with the overall concept of the piece.

The vocalist must know that in the Baroque era composers left out notes in recitatives that singers were expected to sing. At the end of a phrase in a Bach recitative, for instance, if the melody ended in a jump of a third or a fourth, the singer was required to fill in the missing note(s):

But   this   they   said   But   this they   said

Contemporary notation uses many different signs to indicate ornamentation. These signs are not unified by any means, and it is necessary to study them over again with each composer. Generally, ♪ means "to be spoken on pitch" or "half sung." Several forms of glides—either spoken or sung—are indicated by signs resembling these:

Here the vocalist should use some form of small light sound taken from the body of the first note and carry it down to the second. The "siren" exercise is a good way to practice this vocal concept. Once down on the final note, the singer may find it appropriate to add more tone color.

chapter xiii

The Text

Most art songs were initially inspired by a text, a poem that suddenly lit a fire in the mind of a composer. The composer understood something more than the mere words said, and he coveyed that understanding with music. The text of a song is the music's beginning point, the impetus that gave the composer the idea to expand. The composer's idea adds insight into the original poem. How odd it is, then, that so few singers really pay much attention to the words and the poem.

Singers do pay attention to diction and pronunciation, particularly when the song is written in a foreign language. But few of them appreciate the musical attributes of a poem before it has been dressed with music, nor do they often have a feeling for the poem as a whole.

A poem such as James Agee's "Sure on this Shining Night" requires reading over and over again as a poem if the performer is to understand the meaning of the words, the use of the [s], [ŝ], and [ĉ] sounds that have an inner rhythm and the feeling of the poetry itself:

> Sure on this shining night
> Of starmade shadows round
> Kindness must watch for me
> This side the ground.[1]

The [s], [š], and [č] sounds mean something, and the singer must make the meaning as clear as the musical meaning. The next section (the B section in Samuel Barber's setting of the poem) used [l] and [h] for tone quality, a change is thereby indicated. The A section of the poetry (and music)

[1]Agee, James, From *The Collected Poems of James Agee.* Copyright Houghton Mifflin Company. Reprinted by permission of the publisher.

returns in augmented form to a use of [s] and [s], and this time the [w] and [m] sounds are added. These A sections deal with *wish*es and *w*ondering. Therein lies one of the meanings of the poem. The singer that misses the chance to make a subtle but nevertheless decided use of the poet's choice of consonants has missed an opportunity of interpretation. Barber did not miss this opportunity. He placed the words in such a way that they ask to be emphasized lightly but with wonderment.

THE COMPOSER'S INTENTION

In general, the aim of the composer is to set words and music in such a way that the accent of the words coincides with the accent of the music. This is done in subtle ways by such experts as Hugo Wolf, and in less subtle ways by composers who are more concerned with the music than they are with the words. There are times when words are given a good deal more importance than music. The coincidence of musical beat and word beat is often used for comic effect (by Gilbert and Sullivan, for instance). At other times it becomes obvious from the piece that the composer intended the musical beat to be kept, and if that occasioned a misplaced word accent, the skill of the performer would have to ease the situation. Such occurrences happen frequently in strophic material, where each verse is sung to the same melody even though the word structure and the rise and fall of meaning of the different verses do not coincide.

Seldom do the beats of a majority of the words of a song oppose the musical beat. Where this does happen it may be that the composer is thoroughly incompetent or the opposition may be an attempt at humor. There are well-written pieces of music that incorporate this opposition, however, and it is up to the performer to find out why. The follow-ing excerpt from a cantata by Benedetto Marcello is an example. The musical accent occurs on the weak half of beats one and two, whereas the poetic accent falls in the more normal positions of the downbeat and the third beat.

Sorgi Candida Aurora

Benedetto Marcello
Realization and English translation: BKS

What is Marcello trying to say? A thorough study of the piece, the singer attempting first to sing it with the musical accents and then with the poetic ones, brings forth the following insights: When the musical accent is attended to, the lines of the piece are very jerky and the consistent accenting of the weak syllable of the words has a very bumpy and comic effect. In all probability the musical accents spring originally from a dance form, and the length of the accented notes merely represents the length of a dance step rather than the accent of the poetry. The words are not comical in nature; they are a love song. Perhaps if attention were drawn to the accent of the words and the musical accent were ignored, the line would even out into a lyric phrase, but one that would not lose its rhythmical form or interest.

In other words, by thinking of this selection not as da-dá bum, da-dá bum, but rather as da-da long, da-da long, and giving the proper poetic accent, the singer can keep the best of both the music and the poetry, each allowing the other to be heard as a plausible unit. In performance this rather pedantic explanation becomes an easily expressed musical happiness; the line is clear without losing its inner

bounce and gaiety, and the poetry receives a viable reading.

The composer must also deal with the poem's form as well as its content. Barber, as we have seen, follows exactly the poetic form of "Sure on this Shining Night." Strophic songs follow the poetic form, often to the detriment of the poet's intentions. Individuals other than Goethe have felt that strophic poetry should be musically strophic, believing it is the performer's obligation to act out the different stanzas as the poet required, using varied tempi or altering rhythms as the text required. A classical example of a musical distortion of poetic form is the da capo aria of the Baroque period. What poet truly wanted to have his first stanza resung after a contrasting stanza had been sung, and with embellishments? The Romantic era broke down the straight strophic treatment of poetry through composition. In the twentieth century much more than poetic phrases have been dislodged from their original places: words themselves have been broken and used for sound effect in pieces by composers such as Gaburo.

Composers may choose a melody from the inflection of the spoken word for the musical nucleus of a piece:

I'm Nobody

Sergius Kagen
Text: Emily Dickenson

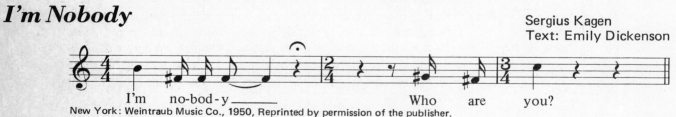

I'm   no-bod-y_____   Who   are   you?

New York: Weintraub Music Co., 1950, Reprinted by permission of the publisher.

These lines are read by Mr. Kagen as:

I'm nobody, Who are *you?*

In contrast, Vincent Persichetti read them as:

I'm *nobody, Who* are *you?*

I'm Nobody

Vincent Persichetti
Text: Emily Dickenson

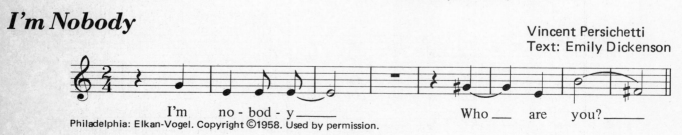

I'm   no-bod-y_____   Who__   are   you?_____

Philadelphia: Elkan-Vogel. Copyright ©1958. Used by permission.

The difference may not seem very exciting until you realize that Mr. Kagen is asking a question quite dramatically, and that his melodic line is

reflected in the upward sweep of his reading of the verse, whereas Mr. Persichetti's reading is more pensive, as can be seen in the downward direction of the vocal line. Both readings are valid, and both have been reflected by the composer in the choice of melody.

Fog

Roy Harris
Text: Carl Sandburg

Here the mood is caught in the right hand and prevails throughout the piece. The line in the poem reads "The fog comes on little cat feet." By interpolating three beats of rest in the middle of the line, the composer has extended the feeling of fog slowly creeping in. The general mood of the piece takes precedence over music and text here.

SCANSION

The term *scansion* is important in the understanding of rhythmic and melodic construction. Scansion is defined by Babette Deutsch as "the detailed analysis of the metrical pattern of lines and stanzas. The terms employed are those of classical prosody."[2] She goes on to establish that these terms are not as applicable to most of the languages used by a singer, particularly English, as they are to classical languages. This is because these languages are qualitative—that is, languages of stress—whereas classical languages were quantitative—languages of length and shortness. However, one can scan a length of English poetry in terms of loud and soft syllables, rather than long and short ones and arrive at a workable plan for the whole.

Ma - ry had a lit - tle lamb

can be translated into music both quantitatively and qualitatively. For instance:

[2]Babette Deutsch, *Poetry Handbook*, 4th ed. (New York: Harper & Row, 1974), p. 158. Reprinted by permission of Harper & Row, Publishers, Inc.

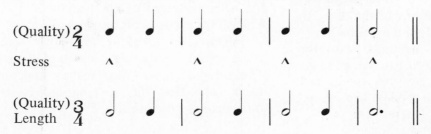

Obviously there are far more subtle ways of accomplishing these extremes (and far more subtle poetry!). These are essentially the means at the composer's command for the translation of the rhythm of poetry into music. Sometimes a composer deliberately distorts or overemphasizes the original scansion to achieve a point:

Mar - y   had   a   lit - tle   lamb

or

Mar - y   had   a   lit - tle   lamb.

THE POET'S INTENTION

Once the composer has chosen the formal, melodic, and rhythmic characteristics of a piece, and the texture she wishes, she begins to shape the text into a song in such a way that the music will enhance the poem. If the singer does not understand the rhythmic makeup of the poem, the form of the poem, and the poet's concept, he may misinterpret the composer's setting of the work. It is as important to understand the poet's intention as it is to understand the musical intention of the composer. Occasionally references to the original poem will disclose that the composer has deleted from or added to it. Sometimes a composer will run lines together that the poet has separated. The performer has to take notice of this problem and attempt to correct it.

Occasionally the wording of the poetry is particularly difficult to understand without the printed word in front of one. Consider, for instance, these lines from Emily Dickinson, "I Felt a Funeral in My Brain":

> Then space began to toll
>
> As all the heavens were a bell.
> And Being but an ear,[3]

Here it is difficult to present the word "Being" as a noun and not a verb. Regardless of the strength of composition, the performer has a problem.

The structure of language combined with the rules of acoustics often leads to problems in performance. Certain vowel sounds, for instance, cannot be sung on high tones because the structure of the vowels will not permit them to exist at a high pitch. When a composer asks a singer to use such tones, the text has to suffer. This is the basic reason why sopranos are generally not as intelligible as baritones. The only recourse a singer has is vowel modification at these points, coupled with good acting ability. Frequently the audience will seem to hear what it cannot in fact hear, because the singer has handled the consonants ably and the vowels are guessed at by the ears of the listeners.

Translations also present textual problems. Poems in their original language have a melodic structure provided by the inflection of the words as well as by the vowel structure and the use of semiconsonants. Noise value provided by the consonants is also of rhythmical worth. All vowels represent two sounds, two distinct formants found in the melodic structure, and are therefore actually two-tone chords. These formants help the poet form a melodic pattern with words. When translation destroys the pattern of vowel sounds and/or the pattern of consonant sounds, as it often does the original intention of the poet is lost. This is the argument advanced by those who oppose recitals in English. The opposite argument stresses communication with the audience, and this side has been enhanced by the professional and artistic English translations on the market today.

Singing and speaking are both sound, both vocal sound. In the art song they come together. The artistic singer must realize that they are a team, and that the text should be treated as thoroughly as the music.

---

[3]From *Poems of Emily Dickinson* (Boston: Little, Brown, 1950) p. 205.

chapter xiv

Repertoire

In the beginning there is a voice teacher who makes descisions. The voice teacher shows the students repertoire, covers those areas that are helpful vocally, knows the songs that will succeed, and leads the students to discover the different phases of musical style and history. Life is pretty easy for the students. At least they are told what to do, like it or not, and they know how to go about doing it. Then there is the day when the selection of repertoire is left up to them. Sometimes it is difficult to know where to begin.

SELECTING REPERTOIRE

Obviously the first variables to consider are the technical demands of the music: its range, dynamics, coloring, shadings, and language; the agility it requires of the vocalist; the suitability of text and style, and any dramatic skills or emotional comprehension needed to perform it. Stretching one's wings in many directions is good if one is in a learning phase, but if picking repertoire with a specific recital or any other type of performance, it is probably better to have most of the technical requirements in hand when one selects material. If compositions are being sought as learning pieces, and if there is no pressure of time for actual performance, then as long as the requirements for range and suitability are met, the sky is the limit. Some of these requirements are self-explanatory:

1. Range: Can you sing the notes well? If you must use either your very low or very high voice, can you do so without making either sound badly and without hurting your voice?
2. Dynamics: Are you capable of producing soft, high singing or low, loud singing if these are required?
3. Coloring: Have you at your command the light and dark tone colors that are needed, and the hushed or vibrant sounds that are called for?
4. Language: Can you translate the song if it is not in English? Can you pronounce the words? Do you understand the text?
5. Suitability of text: Should you sing this song? Is it right for your personality? Is it right for a man (woman) to sing? Do you understand what the poem says, and is the text suitable for your personality and your sound? (For example, it is inappropriate for a sweet lyric soprano to sing chantys, or for a young, itinerant, male preacher to entertain his hosts by singing "My Mother Bids Me Bind My Hair.")
6. Suitability of Style: Some styles sound good in some voices and not in others. The rock-and-roll singer is rarely a singer of lullabies. The young, naive, high soprano voice is not suitable for singing "I Don't Know How to Love Him," a song appropriate to Mary Magdalene and other more worldly types. One may be amused to hear a six-year-old lisp through an ardent love song, but it is not suitable for the age. A voice capable of singing light, fluffy music may have difficulty mustering the tone quality for a dark and ponderous song.

Suitability: it is very important, difficult to define, but, if broached, fatal at the box office and often to the voice. Some opera singers will sing only one type of opera. For example, the Verdi-Puccini school won't sing Wagner, and neither Verdi nor Wagner singers will touch Massenet. Another aspect of suitability in dramatic works is the appropriateness of a voice to the physical stance of its bearer. Tiny sopranos and short baritones have trouble finding "character" parts that are suitable to their statures. On the other hand, a tall soprano will not be cast as Madame Butterfly because of her height.

Repertoire that requires another singer or an instrumentalist may prove to be too costly to use. Singers may not wish to sing a song whose text is embarrassing to them, is uncomfortable, or should not be presented in a small (or large) hall.

Then there are the matters of the key and the arrangement of the music. By necessity publishers usually publish only in one key: medium. Generally *medium* means that the tessitura is either too high or too low. Sometimes the music must be transposed. Sometimes the transposition is awkward to play on the piano or sounds badly at the piano's tessitura or the singer's. Pop music is very frequently not found in the correct key in print. Both pop and art songs are often recorded in an entirely different key than can be found in the published version. The singer must either transpose for the pianist or find another piece. These criteria are fundamental in considering the next questions concerning the choice of repertoire.

Repertoire is garnered from past and present songs. The songs of the future will be the meat of today's students. For this reason, the singer must always be aware of contemporary composition. By the time this repertoire is sung, taste, curiosity, and vocal technique will have to be developed. The young beginner does not have the technique to try very avant-garde material. This is particularly true of music written by composers who are new to their trade and experimenting to find what they can write for vocalists. Such material is often written without the judgment that handles voice with ease and sureness, and consequently is best left to an experienced singer who can help the composer make these judgments and perhaps mediate some of the difficulties of the composition with some concessions.

Contemporary music already in print can be a challenge. This music usually appeared first in recorded form, and listening to the performance on a recording will help one determine the questions of suitability.

Listening to recordings is not a bad thing to do. We learn by imitation, and there is no better way to understand style than to listen to it being produced. There comes a time when curiosity and intellectual independence insist that an opinion of the music be formed from the music itself, without other aural references. Before this point is reached, however, a good deal of eclectic listening—both to recordings and to live performances—must take place in order for one to have sufficient background to make judgments.

Music from the past is found more easily in recordings and in print. This is the music that most schools are primarily concerned with. It is the history that goes into the making of contemporary music, and it constitutes the bulk of the material that is standard for the trade. People who like to listen to vocal music know it and want to hear it. People who sing well are expected to be conversant with it. With the use of a broad outline it is possible to develop some guidelines to the music of the past that will help in the search for suitable literature. The outline that will be the most useful is that of the solo concert literature existing in the main languages of Western music: Italian, French, German, and English.

THE ART SONG

The art song has a long and interesting history. Since the art song provides a good deal of the vocal repertoire, beginning students ought to have some idea of the options available to them within the scope of this genre. A number of books have been written on the subject, as well as countless articles and encyclopedia entries. The intent of this chapter is not to compete with such material (a bibliography at the end of the chapter will give some idea of the sources that can augment this outline) but to provide a framework for the searching of repertoire and a suggestion where choices may be made.

Songs of the Middle Ages

Song, of course, has been with us since the beginning of humankind. It would be difficult to think of a society that did not have some form of a lullaby, a religious ritual, or a dance without the accompaniment of voices. As far as solo song is concerned, one can go back only as far as those songs that have been preserved in notation that today's scholars can interpret. Some music of the Middle Ages falls within this category. The music of that era can be classified as folk music—the music sung by the troubadours, trouvères, and Minnessingers—the music of the educated and sacred music. For centuries folk music formed a very vital background for music considered to be more serious. The latter, in the hands of the educated person, was eventually turned into notation that made in available to history. It wasn't until the nineteenth century in Europe that folk music per se came to be held in esteem by the establishment. During that time the interest in folklore and folk art created by the Romantic movement produced scholarly editions of folk music and performance editions as well. Previously a few scattered songs had made their way into a text or into musical notation. We have, for example, some music from very early mystery plays and some songs that have survived through oral tradition. We also have some songs that found their way into the more structured music of their era, such as masses based on the melodies of folk songs or contemporary church hymns. These masses have saved the melody, if not the original rhythm of the folk tune.

Most of this music is accessible, singable, and thoroughly enjoyable. A good deal of it sounds good with no accompaniment (if you have such courage) or with guitar accompaniment. (Beginning singers please take note: Someone else should play that guitar while you sing; otherwise your basic posture will suffer. Wait until you have conquered the basics of singing and performance before you attempt to accompany yourself.) Modern editions that will be of value to you include the very fine collection *The Oxford Book of Carols*.[1] (*Note*: carols are written not only for Christmas but for the entire religious and secular year.) American collectors such as John Jacob Niles, John Lomax, and Alan Lomax have produced many books, which are readily available in most libraries. Mr. Niles has also written art-song accompaniments for

some of the folk material he has collected. The most popular art-song accompaniments for folk songs are found in the collections of Benjamin Britten. This genre is heartily recommended to all singers.

The works of the trouvères, troubadours, and minnesingers covered a span of centuries. Troubadours flourished in Provence in the twelfth century. Trouvères came a century later in northern France, and the minnesingers appeared in Germany a short time later. These musicians came from many different social levels. They had a counterpart: the jongleur, a traveling musician and acrobat, who supposedly was of a lower class than they. However, this rule did not always apply. Here is a contemporary "job description" of jongleurs:

> *I can play the lute, the violin, the pipe, the bagpipe, the syrinx, the harp, the gigue, the gittern, the symphony, the psaltery, the organistrum, the regals, the tabor, and the rote. I can sing a song well and make tales to please young ladies and play the gallant for them if necessary. I can throw knives into the air and catch them without cutting my fingers. I can do dodges with string, most extraordinary and amusing. I can balance chairs and make tables dance. I can throw a somersault and walk on my hands. . .*[2]

The music of these various singers sometimes found its way into print, as did the names of the composers. Richard the Lion-Hearted, Blondel, and Bernard de Ventadorn are known, among many other names. Some of their songs are known and some are available in contemporary performance editions. They may be a bit strange to our ear, but they are performable. The literature requires a good grasp of languages: few of the surviving pieces are in English, for this was more of a Continental movement, the English making use of the French songs. Bernard de Ventadorn accompanied Eleanor of Aquitaine to England at the time of her marriage, but his songs and hers would have been sung in French.

From Spain of the twelfth and thirteenth centuries came many songs. They probably were sung solo, although it is possible that they were sung in parts. Some of them were collected by Alfonzo X, King of Castile and Leon in the thirteenth century. These songs are available in scholarly editions and are very accessible to the singer.

---

[1]Percy Dearmer, Martin Shaw, Ralph Vaughn-Williams, eds., *The Oxford Book of Carols* (London: Oxford University Press, 1928).

[2]Quoted by Howard D. McKinney and William R. Anderson, *Music in History* (New York: American Book Co., 1954), p. 140.

Their influence runs through Spanish song of subsequent generations.

The followers of St. Francis in Italy produced songs called *Laude*. These are a folk-song approach to church music.

It is impossible to overlook the importance of polyphonic songs in the history of the solo song. In time these songs became more complicated, both in the use of many texts and in musical sophistication. From time to time there was a reaction in favor of simplicity of both text and music, and this in turn strengthened the solo song. There was a constant flow of melodic ideas between the church and the secular world, most of which is not fully documented but is obvious from the manner in which choral music developed. In no case, in the secular field or in sacred music, is the performance practice of these songs completely known. However, most of the songs from the Middle Ages *can* be performed as solo literature with instruments playing the other parts indicated in the scores. The choice of instruments would depend on what is available that is compatible with the singer's voice.

Starting with the fourteenth century, the names of more composers begin to be known to us. We have the music of such masters as Guillaume Machaut. The Italian madrigals composed by men such as Francesco Landini and Jacopo da Bologna contain some material that either was originally written for solo voice or can be so performed. Landini's pieces have a simplicity of melodic line that is very touching.

As the history of song progresses, the availability of the material increases. In England we have the works of John Dunstable. Also from the fifteenth century the choral and solo works of Heinrich Isaac, Josquin Des Prés, Orlando di Lasso, and Guillaume Dufay are all available. These are extremely important composers, and their works are not museum pieces but compositions to be sung. Even though most of this material survives only in scholarly editions, some with contemporary clefs and some not, musicological sources such as the *Harvard Anthology of Music*[3] contain transcriptions performable by the beginning singer. Such transcriptions, along with the scholarly editions, are fertile grounds for exploration. Accessi-

bility depends on the student's musical background and the available library facilities.

Lute Songs

In 1501 a new era for the musical score began with the printing of music by Ottaviano Petrucci in Venice. Easier accessibility to music and the business of selling music then became possible. Today, of course, there is more documentation of the music of that age, since the sources are fuller. Music was written for sale in quantity to talented amateurs among the educated middle class. Part songs and lute songs (sometimes overlapping) became very popular.

In England, a group of composers including William Byrd, John Taverner, Christopher Tye, and Thomas Tallis wrote songs accompanied by string instruments called viols. This was solo literature, and quite a bit of it is available to the singer today. This form was superseded by the lute song, the lute being an instrument more accessible to the singer than a group of viols. The lute song pervaded the Continent and England for many a year. The lute songs of the English composers John Dowland, Robert Jones, William Byrd, Thomas Campion, Philip Rosseter, William Corkine, and many others are all available in modern performance editions. Most of this material is fairly simple as far as pitch and language are concerned, but the rhythmic problems can be telling. Frequently the poet was the singer, instrumentalist, and composer. Under such performance conditions allowances for breathing can be made that are not necessarily notated.

Many lute songs change between a three-pulse and a two-pulse. It is absolutely essential that this rhythmic change be done smoothly and in keeping with the motion of the piece and the flow of the words. Such rhythms generally come from a dance form, as do most rhythms. Since many of these dance forms are totally unfamiliar to our times, it is difficult to spin out their rhythms easily. Lute songs are essentially strophic. That is, many stanzas of poetry (the lutanists were drawn to good poetry) were fitted to the same music that was used for the first stanza of the poem. This also takes some adapting, and it is good to remember, as the history of the strophic song evolves, that it is always the province of performers to accommodate succeeding stanzas to the melody as they see fit.

---

[3]Willi Apel, *Harvard Dictionary of Music*, 2d ed. (Cambridge, Mass.: Belknap Press of Harvard University Press, 1969).

In Spain this type of song was accompanied by the vihuela (de mano), an instrument that is a link between the lute and the guitar. The composers of this material had a wealth of solo songs to draw upon such as those collected by Alfonso X. From this base grew a formidable body of music. Luis Milan produced such a book in 1536. Juan del Encina was another well-known composer of this literature. Many of these works have been collected in various editions.[4] Some of the melodies appear in the contemporary works of Joaquín Rodrigo.

The Italian Baroque

In Germany the lute song was not as important as it was in England and Spain. It was the solo song of the early sixteenth century and the Italian cantata, particularly when it was transformed into the sacred cantata, that started Germany toward her outstanding songs of later centuries. In order to understand some of the background, of the German solo song and cantata, therefore, it is necessary to understand the Italian cantata of that era.

Around 1581 a group of music lovers in Italy formed a group called the Camerata, under the leadership of Count Bardi. It was their desire to maintain a dramatic level of performance that would emphasize the text. They produced music that responded to the melodic line of poetry in what they felt must have been the manner of early Greek theater. Thus the accompaniment was quite thin in texture and the words and their rhythm were very pronounced. Claudio Monteverdi wrote of two practices, a first one that leaned on the contrapuntal style of the Renaissance and a second one, which he and his contemporaries were investigating, where the text dominated the music. As the latter practice developed it was joined to a growing instrumental practice in which a solo instrument was featured against the accompaniment of a keyboard instrument whose bass line was fortified by either a low string instrument or the bassoon. This accompanimental group was called the basso continuo, and its use dominates this age in music. The two parts, solo and bass, polarized the texture, with the middle voices being filled in by the expertise of the keyboard player. The keyboard artist had only the bass line, the vocal line, and

some chord indications in front of him, and from these he was to "realize" the harmony on the harpsichord or the organ.

The Baroque aria and the Baroque song evolved from these beginnings and from the growing interest in opera. Of great interest in the early Baroque are the works of Monteverdi, among which are some beautiful compositions for the solo voice. These are accessible today, and can be found in 'realized" form. They are quite dependent upon the rhythm of the language, and should therefore be studied with the language well in mind, particularly those pieces that stress an unfolding drama. Consequently, some of these compositions are inadvisable for a student unfamiliar with Italian; others are more melodic, and growing familiarity with the language brings them well within the student's grasp.

Early-Baroque composers of opera and song such as Monteverdi, Giulio Caccini, and Jacopo Peri strove to keep the goal of simplicity of music and clearness of text. As the Baroque age progressed, however, the singer's melody, and finally the singer's ability to improvise on that melody, became progressively important. Indeed, throughout the history of performance, aestheticians and theorists who have put forth certain goals for music have had their ideas bent to the accomplishments and the demands of the performers of their works. The pervading interest may be the one at the box office. Or perhaps the performer's goals are more theatrical and such performances are easily enjoyed by the audiences. In any event, as the Baroque era continued the art of the individual performer was expressed in improvisation on a given melody. Melodies, then, were seldom performed as written, but were ornamented.

Another development of the Baroque era was the da capo aria—that is, an aria with an A section, a B section, and a return to the A section. In the A section the singer stated the composer's written intention, probably never completely unornamented. The B section, which consisted of contrasting dramatic or musical content, was then sung—again, probably with some ornamentation. In the return to the A section the singer was expected to embellish the melody with as much ornamentation as style, technique, and ego would permit. The embellishments did have a few rules, most of which must have been broken severely on

---

[4]See, for example, Angles Higini, ed., *Monumentos de la música española* (Madrid: Superior de investigaciones científicas, Instituto Diego Velázquez, 1941).

occasions, judging from critics' remarks about what should *not* be done. Some of the rules were harmonic: no parallel fifths, for instance. Others called for trills at the end of the A and B sections.

The wealth of Italian cantatas currently available to the voice student forms one of the bases for most beginning students' repertoire. The lines are strong and generally do not involve extremes of range or technique, particularly when they are sung without ornamentation. For beginners this approach is just fine, and they should become increasingly familiar with the multitude of literature from this era. The ornamentation can be dealt with later. There are books written during the age itself that give rules and examples for embellishments in the Italian cantata. Caccini's *Le Nuove Musiche* (1602) is readily available in English translation,[5] as is Tosi's *Observations of the Florid Song*.[6]

The Italian cantata was written for the opera singer or the talented amateur, and was performed at private parties or home concerts where the audience may have been of rank but certainly was of education. Opera singers would be requested to perform at these occasions. Therefore, a feeling for the drama in the piece as well as a love of melodic line and the beauty of the lyric voice is necessary in performing this style of music. Composers of the Italian cantata are numerous: Pier Francesco Cavalli, Giacomo Carissimi, Marcantonio Cesti, Giovanni Legrenzi, Alessandro Stradella, Antonio Vivaldi, Agostino Steffani, Giovanni Pergolesi, and Alessandro Scarlatti, to name but a few.

The role of the castrato on the opera stage and the role of the falsettist in Protestant countries had and effect upon the performance and the range of many of these Italian cantatas and songs. The original keys of some of the works written for these voices are somewhat awkward for today's sopranos and tenors and it is occasionally necessary for them to change the key, or at least to know that they will have to make some changes in the feeling of the tone if they use the original key. The compositions are otherwise extremely singable.

The German Baroque

The work of Heinrich Schütz in Germany was influenced by Italian composers. He has left us a number of cantatas, sacred works, and compositions for solo performers. Among his sacred works are the *Kleine geistliche Konzerten*. There are duets and larger vocal combinations for varying voice parts to be found in his compositions.

Schütz's nephew Heinrich Albert was one of a group of composers in Germany who created songs for the solo voice. Albert, Adam Krieger, Andreas Hammerschmidt, and Philipp Erlebach were others. In the last few years a number of excellent recordings of some of their songs have appeared. Many of the songs are extremely well suited to the baritone voice.

J. S. Bach and Handel mark the zenith of the Baroque in the minds of many. The many cantatas of Bach are a treasure of solo as well as choral music. A good deal of the solo material included an obbligato instrument. This proves to be a very worthwhile inclusion in any recital program, since it varies the sound for the audience and is not too costly a gesture to be made by the soloist. Bach's Schemelli choral book is an excellent body of singing literature consisting of his realizations of existing melodies plus a few of his own. A number of the current reprints of this collection of chorales include the few songs that Bach wrote for his wife; these provide excellent material for singers. Breitkopf and Hartel have published all of Bach's work. Many other editions are available.

The English Baroque

Handel's many operas, oratorios, and cantatas are all available for beginners—at least, beginners may pick and choose their way among this rather difficult literature until they find something agreeable to their talents. There are a number of editions of selections from Handel's works. A good library that includes the complete Handel scores will provide even more material. Many of Handel's compositions are in English, although the composer wrote most frequently in Italian, with a very few excursions into his native German. The International Music Company has produced several volumes of Handel arias.

England's most famous composer of the mid Baroque was Henry Purcell. His works include operas and songs, of which a number of modern editions are readily available. Among the other Baroque composers of song in England are Henry Lawes, John Eccles, William Croft, and Thomas Arne. Of course, the towering figure of English composition after Purcell was Handel.

[5]Giulio Caccini, *Le Nuove Musiche*, H. Wiley Hitchcock, ed. & trans. (Madison, Wis.: A-R Editions, 1970).

[6]Tosi, *Observations on the Florid Song*, J.E. Galliard, trans. (London: J. Wilcox, 1926).

The Air de Cour and the French Baroque

The French *air de cour* was a popular counterpart to the English lute song and the Spanish vihuela. The form proliferated throughout Europe and produced "airs" in numerous countries. In France it was influenced by a subject long dear to the hearts of the French: scansion of text. *Musique measuré* with its emphasis on the proper weighting of music to text appears in one set of terms or another throughout the history of French song. Since the French language requires the singer to emphasize by length of note (quantity) rather than by strength of note (quality), as in German and English, it is extremely difficult for one who is unfamiliar with the language to sing it with precision, or to understand the rhythmic flow underneath the musical setting of a French text. The *air de cour* could be extremely sophisticated. At the same time there existed more simple tunes of the *brunette* and *bergerette* type. These songs are somewhat easier to sing. Many of them have simple rhythmic structures and folklike melodies. There is an English collection of these airs[7] and a number of French editions.[8]

Jean Baptiste Lully, an Italian raised and educated in France for the king's service, became a dictator of French style during the latter part of the seventeenth century. He composed many operas and demanded strict adherence to the rhythm of the text. Arias from these operas are available. Marc Antoine Charpentier and his contemporaries in France are apt to be overlooked, since they fall between the heydays of two great composers: Lully and Jean Phillipe Rameau. The latter wrote at the same time as Bach and Handel. His works constitute one of the high points in French opera. Rameau also wrote cantatas that are available.

The popular song form of the late eighteenth and early nineteenth centuries in France was the romance. The most familiar song of this type is Jean Paul Martini's "Plaisir d'amour." Hundreds of other songs were published by such composers as Louis Niedermeyer and Hippolyte Monpou, but very few are readily available to the student today. The romance eventually became bogged down in oversentimentalization and gave way to the *mél-*

odie. This is the term used to describe French art songs of the nineteenth and twentieth centuries. *Mélodies* were greatly influenced by the lieder of Franz Schubert.

The Classic Style

The period of music history that spans the gradual ending of the Baroque, which is associated with the disappearance of the basso continuo, and the rise of the Romantic movement is filled predominantly with the works of the Classic style of Wolfgang Amadeus Mozart, Franz Joseph Haydn, and Ludwig van Beethoven. In England the influence of Johann Christian Bach, son of J. S. Bach, was a telling one. English composers such as William Boyce, Thomas Arne and his son Michael, James Hook and Henry Bishop composed many fine songs, which are becoming increasingly available to the student. Haydn's appearances in England were grand successes during which he produced a number of songs with English texts. George Thomson, a Scottish editor, sold arrangements of folk songs with various instrumentations that were used in home concerts. He convinced (by monetary means) both Haydn and Beethoven to contribute to this group of songs. These songs are available today and have proved to be wonderful program material.

Mozart wrote some very fine songs, which are available in several different collections. A Mozart song can be a good contribution to a program. He composed some excellent songs for beginners as well as songs requiring substantial technical ability.

Beethoven was responsible for the first song cycle, *An die ferne Geliebte*, a group of six songs in continuous form—that is, the songs proceed directly from one to the other without pause and are musically related. Song cycles are not always written in continuous form. Many song cycles, like this one by Beethoven, are collections of songs telling a story. *An di ferne Geliebte* is written for a baritone, and is not an easy piece to sing. There are other songs by Beethoven that are more accessible to the young singer.

The Christian Fürchtegott Gellert lieder (Gellert was a poet of the pietistic school) are quite singable and very programmable. Many of them are attractive and beautiful. The writing of the classical era is very clean. The melodic line is precise and usually very vocal in its sweep and range. The accompaniment is increasingly interesting, but it still keeps out of the singer's way.

[7]Peter Warlock, ed. *French Ayres* (London: Oxford University Press, 1926).

[8]The most accessible of these is J. B. Weckerlin, *Bergérettes.* Sigmund Spaeth, trans. (New York, G. Schirmer, 1913).

A group of German composers created an atmosphere and a demand for the vocal works that preceded the songs of Schubert. The songs of Johann R. Zumsteeg, those of the Berlin School—Carl F. Zelter and Johann Reichardt—and those of Johann J. Loewe are excellent. Many of the same texts that Schubert used a little later were set by these composers. Loewe wrote nineteen volumes of songs, many of which are for bass voice. These songs may be found with a little searching. Many of them are very good for the beginner.

The Romantic Song

Schubert.   Franz Schubert is considered the first of the vocal composers of the Romantic period. His accompaniments are more detailed and have great harmonic interest. Schubert had a more interesting approach to the keyboard than his predecessors. He also had the knack of matching melody and text in a manner that endears him to both the singer and the audience. He wrote over six hundred songs, many of them highlights of the literature. Some are deceptively simple: they read quite easily but they are very difficult to perform, requiring long lines that rise and fall gently. Schubert wrote two long song cycles—*Die schöne Müllerin* and *Die Winterreise*. They do not exhibit the continuous form of *An die ferne Geliebte*, but are collections of songs sung one after the other to tell a story. *An die ferne Geliebte* modulates from one piece to the next. The music never stops. The Schubert cycles are all single songs. The key structure is carefully chosen so that no two songs are in distantly related keys, but follow each other with close key relationships. Although both works were originally written for tenor, the latter is frequently performed by a baritone. Many of Schubert's songs are genuinely for beginners.

Schubert's songs appear in seven volumes in the Peters edition. The International Edition provides English translations in its collections of material from these seven volumes. In addition, many of the songs appear in anthologies. It is important to realize that Schubert's songs are found in several keys in the first three volumes of the Peters edition, but in only one key in the later volumes. International's three-volume collection comes in high and low keys.

The German Romantic Composers.   In the songs of Robert Schumann and Johannes Brahms the accompaniments are more detailed and thicker in harmonic texture. Schumann's piano parts become increasingly important, occasionally consisting of more measures than the singing line. The piano material is as important as the vocal line and relates directly to the content and/or the mood of the poem. Schumann wrote many groups of songs, which are available to sing in their entirety. *Dichterliebe* is a cycle of poems by Heinrich Heine that is usually sung by a man, and *Frauenliebe und Leben* is a group of texts by Adelbert Chamisso for a woman to sing.

Three volumes of songs by Schumann and four by Brahms are published by Peters. In addition the latter set a number of folk songs that are delightful to sing. Both composers were concerned with the quality of the poetry they used, and particularly in the Schumann songs one finds a very high standard in the choice of texts. Their songs are complicated harmonically. Chromatic writing results in the use of many keys and different resolutions. The harmonic texture is thick, and it is difficult for a light voice to sing through the full accompaniment.

The songs of Felix Mendelssohn are few in number but include excellent material. They should not be overlooked. Robert Franz wrote numerous songs, many of them very short and all accessible to the beginner.

In the songs of Richard Strauss the thick accompaniment becomes very lush, heavy and difficult. The songs also make use of the extremes of the singer's range in a way that few composers had done previously. Strauss was another composer who was very selective in choosing his texts.

The Austrian Composers.   In the songs of Hugo Wolf the selection of text and the appropriate choice of rhythms for the delineation of each spoken pattern are handled with extreme care. His method was to saturate himself with the works of a poet and then transform them into music. Consequently, it is possible to hear the difference between his settings of Goethe's poetry and his settings of Edward Mörike's poetry. The musical settings reflect the difference in the poets' styles. There are several volumes of Wolf's work, gathered under the poet's name. These include three volumes of his settings of Goethe's poetry, four volumes of Mörike, and the song cycles *Italienisches Liederbuch* (*Italian Songbook*) and *Spanisches Lieder-*

buch (*Spanish Songbook*). Wolf was a transitional writer whose songs anticipated the work of such twentieth-century composers as Arnold Schönberg, Alban Berg, and Anton Webern.

The early songs of Berg and Schönberg sound much like Strauss. In their later works, however, these two and Webern become intrigued with the sound of a syllable and the placement of text. The musical line is broken, and has many leaps. Rhythm becomes increasingly complex. Pitches and rhythm present great difficulities in these songs, which require maturity, musicianship, musicality, and hard work. Many subsequent twentieth-century songs obviously germinated in the sound and the treatment of text that are found in the works of these three composers. In fact, some contemporary composers of song feel that the text should be used for the sound of the syllable or even for the sound of the individual letter rather than for the understanding of the spoken line or for any meaning that can be conceived from the understanding of that line.

The Rise of the Piano. The small-scale vocal forms of the Romantic age—solos, duets, and so forth—were generally tied to the piano. Accompaniment on that instrument became predominant as the age progressed, and the importance of the piano in the ingredients of song became more obvious. Occasionally an obbligato instrument was added for the enjoyment of all, but even then the piano was the basic accompanying instrument. As we have just seen in the history of the German school, the accompaniment became richer and harmonically full, a thick texture underlying the singer's line. The German composers also added important preludes and postludes to many songs to enhance their structure.

The French Romantics and Impressionists. In the French music of the nineteenth and twentieth centuries there is also an increasing use of the piano. The texture of a song by Claude Debussy is significantly different from that of a song by Strauss, particularly in the later works of these composers. It is in the great works of Debussy and Maurice Ravel that the French song grew into a distinguished vocal accomplishment.

In the beginning of the nineteenth century the song composers of France were predominantly opera composers. The works of Hector Berlioz, which were written earlier than one would suspect from their music, a group of songs—*Les nuit*

d'été—and several single songs that bespeak a growing interest in the form.

As we have seen, the French word for art song is *mélodie*. This term separates art songs from both folk song and popular song. The latter two are called *chanson*. *Mélodies* were written by Charles Gounod, César Franck, Camille Saint-Saëns, Léo Delibes, Georges Bizet, Reynaldo Hahn, and Jules Massenet as well as Berlioz. Massenet was probably the most prolific of that group, but not many of his works are readily available for the singer to buy. Saint-Saëns's work is quite uneven, for he frequently was carried away by poetry that was not worth the effort of setting. With the songs of Henri Duparc and Fauré French vocal literature found a new vigor. These composers were mainly songwriters, and, like their counterparts in the German school, they did much to raise the poetic content and meaning of the art song. Duparc did not write many songs, but those he did were excellent. They are very much like the songs of the German school: rich in harmonics and chromatics and having a thick piano texture underneath. Fauré revitalized the form throughout his life, changing his concept of it and broadening his compositional techniques. His later songs have a sparser texture than his earlier works. The songs of Fauré are very concerned with the shape of the French sentence and the sound of the word. Many of them are quite accessible to beginning singers *if* they are acquainted enough with the sound and the grammar of the language.

Debussy's work is based absolutely on the reading of the text. He wrote many groups of songs that program well in group form, such as *Chansons de Bilitis* and the two *Fêtes Galantes*. Ravel did not write as many songs as Debussy. Some of his songs have orchestra or small chamber accompaniments. This was to become the mark of songs in the twentieth century.

An outstanding twentieth-century composer of the *mélodie* is Francis Poulenc. Most of his compositions are for voice, and his songs tend to be amusing, light, and very vocal. Of course, some are deep, serious, and very vocal. Most of his output was written for the baritone Pierre Bernac.[9]

The Italian Romantics. Italian Romantic songs have not proved as important in the mainstream of

---

[9]Bernac's *The Interpretation of French Song* (New York: Praeger, 1970) is a must for the serious voice student.

song literature as the Italian Baroque outpourings were. The opera remained Italy's main vocal export to the world. There were, however, a few writers of song: Stefano Donaudy and Francesco Tosti contributed to the wealth of Romanticism in forms that are very accessible to the young singer. Ottorino Respighi's works are unequal, but the better ones are very fine indeed. His "Nebbie" can be found in many collections, and many libraries have significant numbers of his compositions. Ildebrando Pizzetti, a composer who lived well into the twentieth century, wrote numerous songs. A few Italian composers in this century have tried to explore the newer methods of composition, sometimes in the harmonic patterns left to us by the Schönberg-Webern school and sometimes in forms of their own. Luigi Dallapiccola is one such composer. His works are very difficult.

The Russian Romantics. The Russian composers of the Romantic school left a substantial song literature. Sergei Rachmaninoff, Peter Tchaikovsky, Anton Rubinstein, Modest Mussorgsky, Alexander Borodin, and Mikhail Glinka all produced beautiful songs. As interest grows in the Russian language this material becomes increasingly available to us. Some translations are available. Most of the songs are quite melodic. Those of Mussorgsky depend heavily on the sound of the Russian language, and frequently do not have the depth when sung in translation that they have when sung in the original. The songs are wonderful material, however, and what is lost in translation is gained in comprehension.

The Nationalists. Songs by such nationalists as the Czech Antonín Dvořák, the Finn Yrjö Kilpinen, and the Norwegian Edvard Grieg are for some reason or other typically sung in German in this country. With the exception of the few Dvořák songs that were originally written to German texts, this makes no sense whatsoever. Good translations in English are heartily recommended. These songs, particularly those of Grieg, are very fine material for the young singer. Those looking for sacred music would do well to consider the ten *Biblical Songs* of Dvořák, for they are oustanding compositions.

The Spanish Romantics. In Spain the compositions of Joaquín Nin have done much to restore some of the melodies of former ages to the concert hall. His arrangements of songs by such composers as Jose Marín are found in a collection entitled *Quatorze Airs Anciens d'Auteurs Espagnols.*[10] The songs are magnificent, and the accompanist must be also. A particular song form known as the *tonadilla* grew out of the Spanish theater. It attracted a good many composers in the early nineteenth century and continued to do so, though in a more sophisticated form, during the twentieth century. Enrique Granados wrote a group of songs in this form, most of them quite attractive to young singers. Manuel de Falla is well known for his group of songs called *Siete Canciones Populares Españolas.* Generally these are sung by a woman and are available in two keys. The works of Joaquín Turina, Granados, Fernando Obradors, Xavier Montsalvatge, and Federico Mompou are all exciting. Mompou wrote a good deal of his songs in Catalan, which may present some problems.

Folk Music and the British Song

The use of folk music is very obvious in the output of late-nineteenth-century and twentieth-century British composers of art song. The group formed by Ralph Vaughan-Williams, Percy Dearmer, Martin and Geoffrey Shaw, and Peter Warlock (Philip Heseltine) was interested in resurrecting the vast amount of British folk music and using it in their compositions. They did much in the way of rearrangements and the resulting works are very usable on the concert stage. Their efforts revitalized the art song for the English and led to the great production of songs by Benjamin Britten and contemporary composers such as Malcolm Williamson, Arnold Cooke, and Humphrey Searle. For a century and a half it had been the theater that satisfied the British, not song literature. Indeed, since the time of Purcell and Handel, with the exception of a few minor composers and the works of Gilbert and Sullivan, British music slept a long and deep sleep. With this renewed interest in folk music the English song has again become popular. The works of Gerald Finzi, Gustav Holst, and Roger Quilter, along with those of composers mentioned above, are very important to the young singer. The several volumes of folk-music arrangements by Britten are most helpful and thoroughly delightful for the listener.

[10]Joaquín Nin, ed., *Quatorze Airs Anciens d'Auteurs Espagnols* (Paris: M. Eschig, 1926).

Latin American Song Composers

In Latin America the songs of Alberto Ginastera, an Argentine composer, are distinguished. Some songs by the Chilean Domingo Santa Cruz can be found. The songs of Heitor Villa-Lobos, a Brazilian composer, are well known, and it is a shame that they are so difficult to buy in this country. Over the past few years there has been a growing concern that the Latin American countries and the United States should share their cultural wealth more advantageously. It is hoped that the Pan American Union, under the direction of composer Juan Orrego Salas, will be able to make music more available to beginning students as well as more musicologically minded individuals.

The Art Song in America

The Nineteenth and Twentieth Centuries. Until this century, the history of the art song in America has been very much tied to the history of the European song. The Founding Fathers had a love for music. The Moravian Brethren, a church that established itself mainly in Pennsylvania, provided a number of songs that were written in German and stemmed directly from the German tradition of the eighteenth century. We find the English tradition being carried on by the few composers of colonial America whom we know about, such as Francis Hopkinson. In colonial New England there were singing schools where itinerant singing teachers taught hymns and general musical works. Among the songs of this period, those by William Billings are particularly noteworthy. Other colonial composers of songs include Justin Morgan and Andrew Law. This literature is becoming more obtainable. During the nineteenth century, musical culture was championed by educators such as Lowell Mason and George Webb. Their songs, which they edited for school use, were primarily instructional. They also wrote for singing groups..

The influences of folk music and the spiritual have been extremely important throughout the history of American music. The Negro minstrelsy of the late eighteenth and the nineteenth centuries reflected blatant racism, but it was also a musical gold mine for writers of popular songs. It is a strong influence that remains in the mainstream of American composition.

Romantic ballads were extremely popular in nineteenth-century America, especially those by Stephen Foster. His songs are simple, but they have a delight that pleases audiences if the melodies are well and tastefully sung. Far too many Americans are not familiar with this material. In fact, Americans do not know Foster's songs as well as Japanese and German schoolchildren do. New editions of Foster's work are currently on the market. His songs are excellent to sing, and, when not overdone, are very programmable. "Slumber My Darling," for instance, is an extremely fine song, and a program can be lightened up considerably by "There Are Plenty of Fish in the Sea."

The art song composers of nineteenth-century America were very much influenced by the German school. In the latter half of the nineteenth century they began to make themselves known: George Chadwick, Horatio Parker, William H. Neidlinger, Amy Marcy Cheney Beach, Ethelbert Nevin, Carrie Jacobs Bond, Sidney Homer, Reginald De Koven, and, the most prominent of the group, Edward MacDowell. Their songs are currently being attended to again, and are becoming increasingly easy to find.

After the First World War a new set of American composers began to produce songs that were influenced more by the French composers of the time. Charles Griffes was one of the earliest of this group. Though he died quite young, he left behind a number of very successful songs. John Alden Carpenter wrote much good material, as did Vittorio Giannini and Ernest Charles. The outstanding American composer of the first half of the twentieth century was Charles Ives, whose musical idiom was years ahead of his time. A successful insurance man, Ives published his own songs and consequently bent neither to public pleasure nor to publishers' demands. Many of his songs are not easy, but once mastered they have unusual and deeply satisfying messages.

Contemporary Composers. The mid-twentieth century has seen several different waves of excellent vocal compostion. Vincent Persichetti, Samuel Barber, and Aaron Copland have presented the voice student with admirable works. Ernst Bacon, Paul Nordoff, Theodore Chanler, Virgil Thomson, Milton Babbitt, Seymour Barab, Alan Hovhaness, Norman Dello Joio, Ross Lee Finney, Douglas Moore, Daniel Pinkham, Michael Horvit, Ezra Laderman, Nicholas Flagello, and David Diamond have written prolifically for the vocalist. The works of Ned Rorem are written primarily for the singer. All of these compositions are excellent, and students need only look to find something suitable to their taste and needs.

With the twentieth century composer we enter the realm of chamber music. It is difficult for beginning students to commit themselves to the rehearsal time necessary for chamber works. Consequently, this wealth of material might well be reserved for a time when the voice is technically in hand. Remember when scheduling chamber works that rehearsal time costs money and that there is never enough of either time or money to complete the job.

Composers writing today in the United States are faced with an economics problem: many of their compositions have been recorded but not published. Consequently, some extremely well written songs cannot be sung by the average student because they are simply not in print. Students interested in the sound of contemporary songs are advised to follow the recent recordings of Composers Recordings, Inc. for guidance.

Musical Comedy and the Popular Song. The American musical comedy has been a source of excellent songs. It is a uniquely American form, leaning heavily on American jazz idioms. The history of the American popular theater could be said to have started with minstrelsy. From there it evolved into the sentimental theater of the late nineteenth century. Since the First World War American musical theater has developed a unique style that is reflected in American popular songs. Many of the songs are excellent vocal material, though deceptively difficult. Often the rhythmic values are extremely surprising, and the tessitura can be frightening. Unfortunately, in much of the music of the 1960s and 1970s the tessitura has become very low. Most sopranos should transpose such material up a third. On the other hand, with the advent in popular music of the semifalsettist, some tessituras have become too high for the baritone to sing easily. Aside from this necessity to transpose, many of the songs of post World War I musical comedy are extremely good repertoire, and should not be ignored by any budding singer.

We are well aware that popular music (as well as some of the more scholarly presentations) is not always sung precisely the way it is notated. Conse-

quently, it is essential to perfect a style of presentation and to be aware of other styles. There is a performance practice in the popular field, and as the history of the field gathers years, singers become less familiar with the sound of preceding generations of songs. Thus, it behooves singers to study, through records, the sound of previous ages in order to find out what the performance practices should be. Performance practice is something that should be studied, for it is inherent in a piece, and before it may be changed or ignored it should be known.

Popular song outside of the Broadway stage is covered very well for the first fifty years of this century in a book by Alec Wilder.[11] The stage works of this half-century are represented in a number of collections, anthologies, and full scores. Composers such as Jerome Kern, Richard Rodgers, Irving Berlin, Harold Arlen, George Gershwin, Frank Loesser, Sigmund Romberg, Vincent Youmans, Burton Lane, Vernon Duke, and Victor Herbert have all contributed outstanding songs to the stage. A group of songs from the 1890s have been published.[12] The *Great Songs* collections of the 1940s, 1950s, 1960s and 1970s are all worthwhile. Frequently, the songs from musical comedies that are found in these and other "selections from" books have keys that are different from those in the scores of the comedies.

This has been a very brief, undetailed outline of the song literature. Much has been omitted. Students should use the names of these composers merely as starting places for finding out what else is in the library, and thus broaden their knowledge of the literature as time and opportunity permit.

SUGGESTIONS FOR FURTHER STUDY

Bernac, Pierre, *The Interpretation of French Song.* New York: Praeger, 1970.

Emmons, Shirlee, and Stanley Sonntag, *The Art of the Song Recital.* Riverside, N.J.: Schirmer, 1979.

[11]*American Popular Song* (New York: Oxford University Press, 1972).
[12]Robert Fremont, ed., *The Gay Nineties* (New York: Dover Publications, 1973).

Hall, James Husst, ed., *The Art Song*. Norman: University of Oklahoma Press, 1953.

Ivey, Donald, *Song, Anatomy, Imagery and Styles*. New York: Free Press, 1970.

MacClintock, Carol, ed., *The Solo Song 1580–1730*. New York: Norton, 1973. (may be used as a performance edition)

Stevens, Denis, ed., *A History of Song*. New York: Norton, 1960.

PERFORMANCE EDITIONS

Italian Baroque Collections

Fuchs, Albert, ed. *Italian Songs of the Eighteenth Century*. International Music Co., 1954. Medium voice.

Jeppessen, Knud, ed., *La Flora*, I-III. Copenhagen: Wilhelm Hanson, 1949. One key; expensive.

Landshoff, Ludwig, ed., *Alte Meister des Bel Canto*, New York: C. F. Peters, n.d., Vols. I and II. One key; mostly for women's voices.

Parisotti, Alessandro, ed., *Anthology of Italian Song of the Seventeenth and Eighteenth Centuries,* Vols. I and II. New York: G. Schirmer, 1894.

——, *Twenty-four Italian Songs*. New York: G. Schirmer, 1894.

English Lute Songs

Warlock, Peter, and Philip Wilson, eds., *English Ayres*. Six vols. London: Oxford University Press, 1931.

German Baroque

Bach, J. S.: various aria books are available through Kalmus, C. F. Peters, and G. Schirmer.

Kagen, Sergius, ed. *Handel Arias*. New York: International Music Co, 1950.

Telemann. New York: Kalmus, n.d. High voice only.

English Baroque

Kagen, Sergius, ed., *Purcell*. 4 vols. New York: International Music Co, 1958/9.

French General Repertoire

Kagen, Sergius, ed., *Forty French Songs*. 2 vols. New York: International Music Co, 1952.

Weckerlin, J. B., ed., *Bergerettes*. New York: G. Schirmer, 1913.

Classical Songs

Christy, Van and Carl Zytowski, eds., *Classic Period Songs*. Dubuque, Iowa: William C. Brown, 1968.

Taylor, Bernard U., ed., *Classic Songs*. Evanston: Summy-Brichard, 1959.

British Twentieth Century

Britten, Benjamin, arr., *English Folk Songs*. London: Boosey & Hawkes, 1943.

Dearmer, Percy, Ralph Vaughn-Williams and Martin Shaw, eds., *The Oxford Book of Carols*. London: Oxford University Press, 1928.

Warlock, Peter, ed., *A Second Book of Songs*. London: Oxford University Press, 1927.

——, *Book of Songs*. London: Oxford University Press, 1924.

Contemporary American Song Books

Taylor, Bernard, ed., *Contemporary American Art Songs*. Bryn Mawr: Ditson, 1977.

——, *Contemporary Songs in English*. New York: Carl Fischer, 1970.

——, *Songs by 22 Americans*. New York: G. Schirmer, 1960.

——, *Songs in English*. Chicago: Carl Fischer, 1970.

Wedding and Church Music

Dvorak, Antonin, *Ten Biblical Songs*. Two vols. New York: International Music Co., 1962.

Pfautsch, Lloyd, ed., *Solos for the Church Year*. New York: Lawson-Gould Music Publishers, 1958.

Spicker, Max, ed., *Anthology of Sacred Song*. Four vols. New York: G. Schirmer, 1902.

Taylor, Bernard, ed., *Solos From the Great Oratorios*. New York: G. Schirmer, 1968. Baritone and soprano volumes available.

Anthologies of Interest for Beginning Students

"The Art Song," in *Music for Millions, Vol. 25*, ed. Alice Howland and Poldi Zeitin. New York: Consolidated Music, 1960.

La Forge, Frank and Will Earhart, eds., *Pathways of Song*. Four vols., particularly vol. III. New York: Witmark, 1938.

Row, Richard D., ed., *Standard Vocal Repertoire*. New York: R. D. Row Music, 1965.

——, *The Young Singer*. New York: R. D. Row Music, 1965. Volumes for each voice part.

Taylor, Bernard, and Mabelle Glenn, eds., *French Art Songs*. Bryn Mawr: Ditson, 1937.

Taylor, Bernard, ed., *German Art Songs*. Bryn Mawr: Ditson, 1947.

——, *Great Art Songs of Three Centuries*. New York: G. Schirmer, 1960.

Songs with Accompaniment

The songs in this chapter have been chosen because they are suitable for young voices. Only, one, Fricker's "Vocalise," is beyond the reach of most beginners. It has been included as a challenge.

The original texts are given. However, each song has a singable English translation. These translations will fit a good many situations better than a foreign language, and it is hoped that they will be used.

This song is a very good learning piece for young men. It is easier to find the right sound on such pieces. The song is written out in a low key. However, chords are given for a higher key, and if you think of the voice part as though it were written in the bass clef in the key of G, you can use the written-in chords and the vocal line to sing in the higher key.

Allessandro Scarlatti
(1660–1725)

Alessandro Scarlatti
Translation: BKS

Gia'll sole dal Gange

Col raggio dorato
Ingemma ogni stelo
e gli astri del cielo
di pinge nel prato.

With sunbeams he showers
Gold over the flowers.
Like stars of the night time
They glow in the sunshine.

Rimprovero

Folk Song
Arranged: Fabio Campana
Translation: BKS

Largo assai — *con molto espress.*

Voice / Piano-forte

Se den - tro l'a - ni - ma Tu mi leg -
Deep in this soul of mine   If you could

ges - si, Se in tan - te la - gri - me Tu mi ve - des - si; Se in tan - te
read there   So man - y tears of mine   If you could see there.   So man - y

la - gri - me, Tu mi ve - des - si, Un sguar-do un pal - pi - to____ A - vrei da
tears of mine   If you could see there.   One lov - ing glance from you____ Hap - p'ly I'd

te. Se in tan - te la - gri - ma Tu me ve - des - si, Un sguar-do un
share.   So man - y tears of mine   If you could see there.   One lov - ing

pal - pi - to a - vre - i da te.
glance I would so hap - p'ly share.

Se l'al - ba è can - di - da, Per te so - spi - ro, Se den - sa
When dawn a - wakes the day My heart's still sigh - ing. All through the

te - ne - bre, Per te de - li - ro, Se den - sa te - ne - bre, Per te de -
night I pray To stop my cry - ing. All through the night I pray, To stop my

li - ro, Mia vi - ta e spa - si - mo,___ D'a - mor de fe. Se in tan - te
cry - ing. My life is emp - ti - ness___ When we're a - part. So man - y

Royal Edition, Songs of Italy, London: Boosey and Co. n.d. p. 166.

This is a good learning song for women's voices. Most voices will feel comfortable in this key.

Attributed to
Giovanni Battista Pergolesi

Se tu m'ami, se sospiri

Attributed to
Giovanni Battista Pergolesi
Translation: BKS

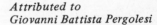

che so - let - to *Io ti deb - ba ri - a - mar,* Pa - sto - rel - lo,
lieve my fa - vor Should belong to on - ly you, Sim - ple fel - low

sei sog - get - to *Fa - cil - men - te a t'in - gan - nar,* Pa - sto - rel - lo,
soon you'll sa - vor De - cep - tion since I shan't be true; Sim - ple fel - low,

sei sog - get - to *Fa - cil - men - te a t'in - gan - nar.*
soon you'll sa - vor De - cep - tion since I shan't be true,

Fa - cil - men - te a t'in - gan - nar. *Bel - la ro - sa por - po - ri - na*
De - cep - tion since I shan't be true. Love - ly ros - es fresh and bloom - ing

Og - gi Sil - via sce - glie - rà, *Con la scu - sa del - la spi - na*
Sil - via can find ev - 'ry day, When the thorns start in - trud - ing

Ma se pen-si che so-let-to Io ti deb-ba ri - a-mar, Pas-to-rel-lo,
But if you be-lieve my fa-vor Should be-long on-ly to you, Sim-ple fel-low

sei sog-get-to Fa-cil-men-te a t'in-gan-nar, Pa-sto-rel - lo,
soon you'll sa-vor De-cep-tion since I shan't be true, Sim-ple fel - low,

sei sog-get-to Fa-cil-men-te a t'in-gan-nar, Fa-cil-men-te a t'in-gan-nar.
soon you'll sa-vor De-cep-tion since I shan't be true, De-cep-tion since I shan't be true.

24 Italian Songs, New York: G. Schirmer, 1894. p. 68.

Un moto di gioja

Wolfgang Amadeus Mozart
Text: Lorenzo da Ponte?
Translation: BKS

Allegretto moderato

Un mo-to di gio-ja mi sen-to nel pet-to, che an-nun-zia di
E-mo-tions of joy in my heart are now beat-ing, that tells me of a

Ah! qu'il fait beau

Brunette
Arranged: J. B. Weckerlin
Translation: BKS

Andantino non troppo lento (♩ = 96)

Ah! qu'il fait beau dans ce bo - ca - ge!
Ah! it is pleas - ant in the flow - ers!

Ah! que le ciel donne un beau jour!
Ah! how the sky is soft with light.

Le ros - si - gnol, sous ce ten - dre feui - la - ge,
Night - in - gales sing from their leaf - trem - bling bow - ers

Chante aux é - chos son___ doux___ re - tour!
Songs that will ech - o through___ the night.

Ce beau sé - jour, ce doux__ om - bra - ge,
Beau - ti - ful__ day, beau - ti - ful__ ho - urs

Ce beau__ sé - jour nous in - vite à l'a - mour.
Beau - ti - ful__ day bring - ing love in your sway.

Weckerlin, Jean Baptiste. *Echos du Temps Passe.* Paris: Durand, n.d., Vol. II, p. 42.

In stiller Nacht

Folk Song
Johannes Brahms
Translation: BKS

Langsam

1. In stil - ler Nacht, zur er - sten Wacht, ein
1. As eve - ning light, turns to the night a

molto legato

110

ich sie all' be - gos - sen. 2. Der
si - lent - ly I lan - guish. *2. The*

molto legato
pp *p*

schö - ne Mon will un - ter - gon, für Leid nicht mehr mag
love - ly moon has set too soon, it can - not stand my

dolce

schei - nen, die Ster - ne - lan ihr Glit - zern stahn, mit
sigh - ing, The small - est star twink - les a far and

dolce

mir sie wol - len wei - nen. Kein Vo - gel sang noch
joins me in my cry - ing. No birds do sing of

più f

Freu - den klang man hö - ret in den Lüf - ten, die
hap - pier things to fill the air with glad - ness The

f *dim.*

Brahms, Johannes. Folk Song's, New York: International Music Co., 1950. Vol. 2, p. 42

Ich halte treulich still

J. S. Bach
Text: J. H. Till
Translation: BKS

Bach, J. S. Geistliche Lieder und Arien. Wiesbaden: Breitkopf und Härtel, n.d., p. 30.

D'rum dank' ich meinem Gott und halte treulich still;
es gehe in der Welt, wie es mein Gott nur will.
Ich lege kindlich mich in seine Vaterhand
und bin mit ihm vergnügt in meinem Amt und Stand.

Thus thanks I give my God and cling to my love of Him.
And fate may change my days through God's beloved whim.
I lie down childishly in His safe Father's care.
And am with Him content through all my daily fare.

Wie des Mondes Abbild

Robert Franz
Text: Heinrich Heine
Translation BKS

bo - gen: al - so wan-delst du, Ge - lieb - te, still und si - cher, und es zit - tert nur dein
por - tion; So do you be - lov - ed wan - der, Still and sure - ly, and then trem - bles, Your re -

Ab - bild mir im Her - zen, weil mein eig - nes Herz er - schüt - tert.
flec - tion through my be - ing, and my heart the sea re - sem - bles.

Franz, Robert, *Ausgewählt Lieder*. Frankfort: Peters, n.d. p. 32.

Wie des Mondes Abbild (Low Voice)

Robert Franz
Text: Heinrich Heine
Translation: BKS

Larghetto tranquillo
Liese, innig, sanft getragen

Wie des Mon - des Ab - bild zit - tert in den wil - den Mee - res -
As the moon's re - flec - tion trem - bles On the waves of the wild

wo - gen, und er sel - ber still und si - cher wan - delt an dem Him - mels -
o - cean, And it si - lent, still and sure - ly Wan-ders through the heav - en's

bo - gen: al - so wan - delst du, Ge - lieb - te, still und si - cher, und es zit - tert, nur dein
por - tion; So do you be - lov - ed wan - der, Still and sure - ly, and then trem - bles Your re -

Ab - bild mir im Her - zen, weil mein eig - nes Herz er - schüt - tert.
flec - tion through my be - ing, And my heart the sea re - sem - bles.

Franz, Robert, *Ausgewählt Lieder.* Frankfort: Peters, n.d. p. 45.

O sah ich auf der Heide dort

Robert Franz
Text: Robert Burns
Translation: von Freilligrath

Allegro molto agitato

O säh ich auf der
O wert thou in the

Hei - de dort im Stur - me dich, im Stur - me
cauld blast, On yon - der lea, on yon - der

teilt ich ja, gern teilt ich ja! O,
share it a', to share it a'. Or

*bield = shelter.

wär ich in der Wü- ste, die so braun und dürr, die so
were I in the wild- est waste, Sae black and bare, sae

braun und dürr, zum
black and bare, The

Pa- ra- die- se wür- de sie, wärst du bei mir, wärst
des- ert were a Par- a-dise, If thou wert there, if

du bei mir! Und wär ein Kö- nig
thou wert there; Or were I Mon- arch

ich, und wär die Er - de mein, du wärst in mei - ner
o' the globe, Wi' thee to reign, The bright-est jew - el

Kro - ne doch der schön - ste Stein, der schön - ste Stein.
in my Crown Wad be my Queen, wad be my Queen.

Franz, Robert, *Ausgewählt Lieder*. Frankfort: Peters, n.d. p. 9.

Mein Schatz ist auf der Wanderschaft

Robert Franz
Text: Karl Wilhem Osterwald
Translation: BKS

Allegretto con grazia

Mein Schatz ist auf der Wan - der - schaft so
My love has been a - wan - der - ing for -

lan - ge, Gott weiss wo - her er nimmt die Kraft zum Gan - ge;
ev - er, God knows what strength he needs for this en - deav - or;

Ihr spre-chet wohl: "Ich such dir aus ein'n an - dern!"
She speaks to me, "I wish you'd find an - oth - er."

Frau Mut -ter, da wird nie was draus! Vom Wan - dern wird er zur rech - ten
Dear Moth - er, no one else is worth the both - er. He will quite soon be-

Stun - de ruhn und bald sein letz - te Rei - se tun und keh - ren mir zum
gin to feel That t'wards his home - land he should steal Re - turn - ing to his

Glü - cke zu - rü - cke.
trea - sure with plea - sure.

Ich liebe dich

Ludwig van Beethoven
Text: Karl Friedrich Herrosee
Translation: BKS

halt' uns Bei - de.
grant His plea - sure.

Beethoven, Ludwig. *Ausgewählte Lieder.* New York: Peters, n.d. p. 147.

Slumber My Darling

Written and Composed by
Stephen C. Foster
1826-1864

Poco Adagio

1. Slum - ber my dar - ling, thy moth - er is near   Guard - ing thy dreams from all
2. Slum - ber my dar - ling, till morn's blush - ing ray   Brings to the world the glad

ter - ror and fear.   Sun - light has past   and the twi - light has gone,
tid - ings of day: Fill the dark void   with thy dream - y de - light—

Slum - ber my dar - ling, the night's com - ing on. Sweet vi - sions at -
Slum - ber, thy moth - er will guard thee to - night. Thy pil - low will

tend thy sleep Fond - est, dear - est to me,
sa - cred be From all out - ward a - larms;

While oth - ers their rev - els keep, I will watch o - ver thee.
Thou, thou art the world to me In thine in - no - cent charms.

Slum - ber my dar - ling, the birds are at rest, The wan - der - ing dews by the

flowers are ca - ressed, Slum - ber my dar - ling, I'll wrap thee up warm, And

pray   that the an - gels   will   shield   thee from   harm.

Foster, Stephen. *Slumber My Darling*. New York: Horace Walters, 1862.

Vocalise

For Barbara Kinsey
Peter Racine Fricker

Adagio

p(Ah)

Reprinted by permission of the composer.

New Moon

Barbara Kinsey Sable

New moon through mi-mo-sa tree I sat with my love and he sat with me, we dreamed the dreams of things to be my love and I and mi-mo-sa tree. New moon through mi-mo-sa tree Next to my love, my love next to me, and all of the dreams we i-ma-gined to be We have to-night by mi-mo-sa tree.

New moon through mi-mo-sa tree, my love and I — and mi-mo-sa tree.

The Bell-Man

Edmund F. Soule
Text: Robert Herrick

Allegretto (♩ = c. 96)

From noise of scare-fires rest ye free, From mur-ders *Be - ne-

di - ci - te! From all mis-chanc - es that may fright your pleas-ing

slum - bers in the night: Mer - cie se - cure ye all, and

*Pronounced Be-ne-diss'-i-tee.
(God bless us!)

keep____ The Gob - lin from ye while ye sleep.

Past one-o'- clock, and al-most two, My Mas-ters all, — My Mas - ters all, — My

Mas - ters all _____ good day to you!

Sometimes I Feel Like a Motherless Child

Spiritual
Arranged: J. Rosamond Johnson

long ways ___ from home. _____

Edelweiss

Words by Oscar Hammerstein 2nd
Music by Richard Rodgers

Moderato

Refrain (Slowly, with expression)

E - del - weiss, E - del - weiss,

Ev - 'ry morn - ing you greet me.

Bless my home-land for-ev - - er.

ev - er. ev - er.

Optional Final Ending

Oh, What a Beautiful Mornin'

Words by Oscar Hammerstein 2nd
Music by Richard Rodgers

Tempo di Valse

looks like it's climb - in' clear up to the sky.
ol' weep - in' wil - ler is laugh - in' at me.
lit - tle brown mav' - rick is wink - in' her eye.

mf a tempo

poco rit.

Refrain:

Oh, what a beau - ti - ful morn - in', Oh, what a

mp a tempo

beau - ti - ful day. _____ I got a beau - ti - ful

feel - in' Ev - 'ry - thing's go - in' my way. _____

1.
2. All the
3. All the

p

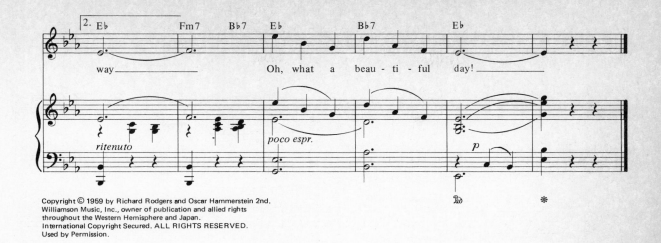

way_____ Oh, what a beau - ti - ful day!_____

ritenuto *poco espr.* *p*

The Cloths of Heaven

Thomas F. Dunhill
Text: W. B. Yeats

Moderato, ma con moto

p semplice

Voice

Piano

p legato, sempre semplice *pp*

Had

I the heaven's em - broid - ered cloths, En - wrought with gold - en and

sil - ver light, The blue and the dim and the dark cloths Of

chapter xv

Responsibilities and Expectations

RESPONSIBILITIES

Students have several areas of responsibility to their voices and to their teachers. Since the voice is their bodies, it should not be mistreated. One does not jump up and down on a Stradivarius violin and expect it to produce good noises. To mistreat the body is equally stupid. Frequently the young disregard pearls of wisdom from ancient and doddering professors because at twenty-three they can sit up all night and sing the next day. But beware of thirty, or even twenty-nine! The vocal folds will take only so much abuse. A young body may recover so that the strain does not show until much later, when it is apt to be too late. Voice production requires work, and it requires muscular alertness. The following abuse either the vocal processes themselves or the body that supports them:

1. technical abuse, or wrong singing, in general; singing without proper support
2. poor health
3. smoking
4. fatigue
5. emotional tension
6. overeating and overdrinking
7. insufficient exercise
8. screaming and *loud talking*, particularly excessively high- or low-pitched, unsupported talking
9. singing on a sore throat
10. talking too low

Remember, at the time of heavy rehearsing it is not particularly the extra singing that will cause vocal fatigue, but the body fatigue that results from additional hours of singing under tension and the additional hours needed to make up work that should have been done during the rehearsal time. Hours of rehearsing generally find the student singer very tired about halfway through. The support goes, and the rest of the rehearsal is poorly sung. It makes sense, then, to remember when your extra rehearsing will be, and to be sure that the rest of your work is out of the way to allow for that extra time.

It is better to stop practicing than to sing poorly: why practice mistakes?

The student who intends to "go for broke" as a singer had better start limiting late hours now, and learn how to manage daily living with a practice schedule and how to say no to invitations to loud, late, and smoky parties.

Singers should pay as much attention to their speaking voices as they do to their singing. They should be properly supported and used in the proper range and at the proper dynamic level. A singer should also learn to be silent at times!

"Going for broke" is difficult to define. The verbal commitment to do so is fairly easy to make. But where do you begin? Unfortunately, the schedule and the manner in which this decision is made is up to the singer—not his teacher, not his manager, but the singer himself. He must make up the schedule, he must keep it in spite of disappointments and economic tribulations, and he must discover what the decision consists of for him and how to effect it. It is hoped he will have some help, and with luck the help will be knowledgeable. Such luck comes in the form of a good manager, a number of opportunities to sing in public where mistakes may be made and ways of performance tried, helpful advice from good people, including a teacher, and even financial help in the form of scholarships or grants.

The greatest responsibility is to the music. It is the singer's responsibility to produce the best tone, the best musical insight, with the best musicianship and the best understanding of the text as is possible at any given stage of development. He will also be called on to act well on the stage. This is the responsibility of the teacher, the student, and the performer. It is our reason for being in music.

EXPECTATIONS

A student should look for the following from a voice teacher:

1. technical ability to teach voice, and several different vocabularies to explain the same thing
2. a definite idea of vocal sound
3. musicality and muscianship
4. patience
5. concern for each student
6. enthusiasm for music and for vocal sound

A teacher should look for the following in a student:

1. talent (the cheapest item on the list)
2. musicality
3. musicianship
4. performability; can the student communicate over the lights?
5. the ear that will hear and correct vocal sound by instinct, or at least will learn to do so
6. *will (determination)*
7. the ability to learn and retain vocal technique
8. *work*

A singer must attain endurance. Often what appears to be good luck—a golden opportunity at an early age—turns out to be bad luck. Young singers who have not learned vocal endurance or who have not developed the tools to substantiate a good technique cannot continue in a career. Success often demands being at the right place at the right time with just the right technique and style and just the desired repertoire. Endurance requires a backlog of these things. Growing family or financial obligations, or sheer running down of the battery of enthusiasm in the wake of persistent ill fortune, ill health, or lack of opportunities, force the best of singers to leave the field. A great deal of good, well-practiced material is wasted thereby. Those who do succeed have little reason to feel superior. Honest success recognizes responsibility toward the profession and toward music. It also knows, most humbly, that there are others who sing, act, persevere, and study equally well, and possibly better.

The singer who has had "luck" or found a "break" had better have the technique to substantiate it, or she will find no future in spite of her fortune. One must constantly train and retrain in order to meet the demands of the field. Practice becomes more than a habit: it is a way of life. In other words, "luck" may be little more than good training, a prepared singer, and a background of endurance—plus the great fortune of a good opportunity to be heard.

At the beginning of this book it was stated that a book cannot teach you to sing. That is very true. With this book in hand you may progress to a teacher in whom you have placed your trust and musical respect and you will attempt to find a sound. That teacher, as many teachers do, will have a theory or an order by which he or she teaches voice. That theory will probably be a most correct theory. The teacher will tell you what to do to achieve such and such a sound, and will try to explain that you should feel such and such a way in order to produce a sound. Most of these theories for helping you find your voice will be correct. But all of the knowledge of the "buttons" you must push and pull, stretch and relax, expand and support in order to sing will not teach you the "vocal sound." The vocal sound is learned by an experienced ear (yours experienced through learning) listening to its own body produce a sound capable of expressing in music the artistry that will help to order the questions and answers of life. Just as a good teacher is a pair of acute ears with many ways of saying the same thing, a good singer has trained his ear to hear the sound that is his sound and has trained his mind to adapt that sound in as many ways as are necessary to convey the art of music, vocal music.

It is hoped that your teacher and finally your own ears—for your own ears are the best and most constant teacher you have—will be able to lead you to that sound, and that those same ears will recognize it as the sound that is meaningfully yours. When you have found it, use it to make music for you and for others, so that life for all of us may be a little bit more pleasant and meaningful.

Appelman, D. Ralph, *The Science of Vocal Pedagogy*. Bloomington: Indiana University Press, 1967.

Coffin, Berton, *The Sounds of Singing*. Boulder, Colo.: Pruett Press, 1977.

Delattre, Pierre, "Acoustics of Vowels," *Eric*, No. 025182, 1968, pp. 41-63.

——, "The Physical Attributes of Speech," *Eric*, No. 010231, 1966, pp. 61-82.

Gray, Henry, *Anatomy*. New York: Bounty Books, 1977.

Husler, Frederick, and Yvonne Rodd-Marling, *Singing: The Physical Nature of the Vocal Organ*. London: Faber & Faber, 1965.

Klein, Joseph, and Ole Schjeide, *Singing Technique: How to Avoid Vocal Trouble*, Chap. I. Princeton, N. J. Van Nostrand, 1967.

Large, John, and Thomas Shipp, "The Effect of Certain Parameters on the Perception of Vocal Registers," *NATS Bulletin*, 26, no. 4 (October 1969), 12-15.

Luchsinger, Richard, and Godfrey Arnold, *Voice—Speech—Language*, trans. Evelyn Robe Finkbeiner, Belmont, Calif.: Wadsworth, 1965.

Manén, Lucie, *The Art of Singing*. London: Faber Music, 1975; Bryn Mawr: Theodore Presser, 1976.

Meano, Carol, and Adele Khoury, *The Human Voice in Speech and Song*. Springfield, Ill.: Charles C Thomas, 1967.

Rubin, Henry, "Role of the Laryngologist in Management of Dysfunctions of the Singing Voice," *NATS Bulletin*, 22, no. 4 (May 1966), 22-f.

Smith, Ethel Closson, "An Electromyographic Investigation of the Relationship Between Abdominal Muscular Effort and the Rate of Vocal Vibrato," *NATS Bulletin*, 26, no. 4 (May/June 1970), 2-f.

Sonninen, Aatto, "Paratis-gram of the Vocal Folds and the Dimensions of Voice," *Proceedings of the 4th International Congress of Phonetic Sciences*, Helsinki, 1961, pp. 250-58.

Van Den Berg, J., "Vocal Ligaments Versus Registers," *NATS Bulletin*, 20, no. 2 (December 1963) 16-31.

Vennard, William, *Singing: The Mechanism and the Technic*, 4th ed. New York: Carl Fischer, 1967.

Index